unKingdom

unKingdom

Repenting of Christianity in America

SECOND EDITION

MARK VAN STEENWYK

CASCADE *Books* · Eugene, Oregon

UNKINGDOM
Repenting of Christianity in America
Second Edition

Scriptures taken from the Holy Bible, New International Version®, NIV®. Copyright
© 1973, 1978, 1984, 2011 by Biblica, Inc.™ Used by permission of Zondervan. All
rights reserved worldwide. www.zondervan.com The "NIV" and "New International
Version" are trademarks registered in the United States Patent and Trademark Office
by Biblica, Inc.™

Cascade Books
An Imprint of Wipf and Stock Publishers
199 W. 8th Ave., Suite 3
Eugene, OR 97401

www.wipfandstock.com

PAPERBACK ISBN: 978–1–5326–7677–2
HARDCOVER ISBN: 978–1–5326–7678–9
EBOOK ISBN: 978–1–5326–7679–6

Cataloguing-in-Publication data:

Names: Van Steenwyk, Mark, 1976–, author.

Title: unKingdom : repenting of Christianity in America / Mark Van Steenwyk.

Description: Eugene, OR : Cascade Books, 2020 | Includes bibliographical references.

Identifiers: ISBN 978–1–5326–7677–2 (paperback) | ISBN 978–1–5326–7678–9 (hard-
cover) | ISBN 978–1–5326–7679–6 (ebook)

Subjects: LCSH: Jesus Christ—Kingdom. | Repentance—Christianity. | Christianity and
culture. | Christian anarchism.

Classification: BT800 .V36 2020 (paperback) | BT800 .V36 (ebook)

Manufactured in the U.S.A.   02/17/20

Contents

A Preface to the Second Edition

The first edition of this book (previously titled *The UNkingdom of God: Embracing the Subversive Power of Repentance*) was published by InterVarsity Press in 2013.

Perhaps you're wondering: Why a new edition? Why a new publisher?

The answer to that question begins in 2015. InterVarsity Press is an extension of InterVarsity Christian Fellowship. In early 2015, InterVarsity Christian Fellowship issued a theological edict against same-sex relationships, sex before marriage, divorce, masturbation, etc. In fall 2016, InterVarsity made it plain that every single employee was expected to affirm the statement. Those that would not were expected to quit.

Evangelical organizations have been notoriously inhospitable to LGBTQ+ folks. But this decision from InterVarsity (which up until this point had the reputation of being the most tolerant and thoughtful of the major Christian campus ministries) took things to a whole new level of inhospitality. Even the queer-adjacent were subject to exclusion.

To be fair, at least InterVarsity was being consistent. I, however, was not consistent. I knew when I published with IVP that I was working with a homophobic organization. However, my intended audience for unKingdom was (and probably still is) evangelicals. It made the most sense to publish with an evangelical publishing company.

I still believe that it was a necessary compromise. However, when InterVarsity took this stance, I knew I couldn't compromise any longer. How could I write a book about repenting from American Christianity and remain silently complicit in a gross act of oppression done in the name of Jesus?

In fall 2016, I joined a group of IVP authors in publicly condemning the actions of our publisher. But that didn't seem like a strong enough stance. And so, in early 2017, I bought back the remaining copies of my book, effectively taking it out of print. As far as I know, I am one of only two authors who took this approach (the other being Jamie Arpin-Ricci).

Shortly thereafter, someone from Wipf and Stock approached me about publishing a 2nd edition.

There are only a few noticeable changes to this book, each significant in their own way:

- IVP wouldn't let me use any cusswords. Wipf and Stock, however, are ok with well-placed cusswords.

- I've omitted the original chapter 3: "Repenting of Plastic Jesus." It was a weak chapter that disrupted the flow of the book.

- I've added a group discussion guide at the end of each chapter because good theology comes from community.

There are other changes as well . . . but they are changes that readers of the first edition are likely to miss. Subtle word changes here. A new sentence there. Overall, the book has a much better flow and style.

Introduction:
Waking from the American Dream

The author at the age of seventeen.
For those interested, the hat band is made of rattlesnake.

IN MY SENIOR PICTURE, I'm wearing a red-white-and-blue rodeo-style shirt, a cowboy hat, and cowboy boots. My nickname in high school was "Garth."

I was the only kid in town who wore a cowboy hat to school every day. There was one other kid—he was on the hockey team and had a mullet—who wore a hat to school from time to time. But he was legit; he rode horses. I was just a poseur. My garb was like a costume trying to communicate something: I was America.

To me, the American Dream was a pure thing. Historian James Truslow Adams coined the phrase in his book *The Epic of America*, when he referred to it as "that American dream of a better, richer, and happier life for all our citizens of every rank, which is the greatest contribution we have made to the thought and welfare of the world. That dream or hope has been present from the start. Ever since we became an independent nation, each generation has seen an uprising of ordinary Americans to save that dream from the forces which appeared to be overwhelming it."[1]

That dream meant that every citizen could achieve whatever was within their ability. It meant that all people, no matter the situation they were born into, could be free to pursue comfort and happiness without the constraint of others. And it was the job of the US to bring that dream to the rest of the world, even if it meant fighting against those who resisted that dream.

It was this dream that made America great. It was our collective dream for all people, it was God's dream. God desired that all people could be free. Jesus died to free us from sin, and soldiers died to free us to live into the American Dream. It seemed to me that God had chosen the United States of America to be his vessel for pouring out blessing upon the world.

When I was seventeen, my friends and I went to a local amusement park—Valley Fair. After a day of stuffing my face with fried food (which I almost hurled while riding Excalibur—their largest roller coaster at the time), we settled in for the evening entertainment. They had a musical extravaganza complete with lasers and fireworks.

The last song they played was "God Bless the U.S.A." If you aren't familiar with this song, Google it. It is perhaps the most epically patriotic song ever written. It's an old song, but not an *oldie*—it gained popularity after the first Gulf War. There was even a push to make it the national anthem.

As the lasers cut patriotic images into the smoky sky, my friends and I sang our hearts out. Lee Greenwood's song is made for singing. Being a Minnesotan, I eagerly awaited the part where good ol' Lee belted out this stanza:

> From the lakes of Minnesota
> to the hills of Tennessee . . .

When he got to the refrain ("I'm proud to be an American, where at least I know I'm free . . .") I could no longer sing along. With tears in my eyes and a sob in my throat, I broke down weeping. I was overwhelmed with a sense of gratitude and pride. I wept as the song played out. And I continued to weep as the fireworks began to fill the night sky. It was like a mystical experience.

---

1. Quoted in Cullen, *American Dream*, 4.

I loved America. I was America.

I was optimistic about the future. Although I was the youngest of six in a lower-middle-class family, I got good grades and scored well on the ACT. My plan was to join the military to pay for college, and go from college to law school and then enter into politics. I dreamed of running for president in 2024.

But I wasn't just patriotic. I was devoutly Christian. I gave my life to Jesus at Bible camp when I was fourteen years old. That was the summer I met my future wife, Amy. We were virgins when we married. I was the embodiment of American Christian fidelity.

But things change.

Today, my wife, son, and I live in an intentional community (which is just a fancy term for commune). We formed this community, the Mennonite Worker (formerly called Missio Dei), in 2003. Ours is the sort of community that protests war, gets food out of dumpsters, rides bicycles, grows our own veggies, and refers to America as an "empire." We are modern-day hippies. In high school, I would have hated me.

When I reconnect with friends from my younger years, they sometimes ask, "What happened?"

Long story. Let's go back to 1990. I was fourteen years old and attending a Bible camp in rural Minnesota called Camp Joy. I was an unpopular kid in school and was completely worthless around girls. If puberty is an awkward time of life for an emerging man, then my puberty was in puberty. To make things even more awkward, it was high school week, so most of the campers were older than me.

But something unexpected happened in that week at camp. In the midst of my feelings of awkward alienation, I felt connection. A few people I met that week would become longtime friends. In fact, I met Amy during that week. But the most unexpected thing was what happened on the final night of camp.

It was the custom of Camp Joy to have a campfire on the final evening, right after the talent show. In those days, the fire was made down by the lake, right next to the chapel. For many, it was the best time of the week: fifty teenagers, gathering in a circle around a crackling campfire as the waves of Star Lake gently lapped the shore.

The goal was to sit at the campfire with a special someone; many new couples had formed that week. Some had already dated and broken up. I was one of the typical campers—I wasn't dating anyone, so I sat with friends. I had had a crush on a girl all week but never got up the courage to ask her out.

As the campfire blazed, a counselor led us in songs with their slightly-out-of-tune guitar. Between songs, campers were encouraged to share testimonies. The testifier would walk up to the center of the group, right in front of the fire, and then tell a story about how their life had been changed by God. When they were done sharing, they would pick out a stick from an old cardboard box and throw it into the fire. It was a little ritual meant to express that whatever had been shared was being offered up to God.

On this particular summer evening, most of the stories were depressing. Everyone shared melancholy stories of death and disappointment, of loss and regret. Several campers spoke of the passing of a grandparent. One told about how his father used to beat him so he and his mother had to flee. Some told less intense stories about the death of a pet or the ending of a relationship. A few went into strangely vivid detail about past sins from which Jesus had delivered them.

In the midst of it all, I suddenly felt overwhelmed with a feeling that I had never before experienced. It was as though their pain was my pain. I felt connected to the suffering of the other campers and, even more confusing, to the suffering of the world. Nothing in my life had prepared me for that experience. It wasn't merely a feeling of empathy—it felt cosmic. It didn't feel abstract, either; I felt as though I could feel the woundedness of the world. And the most painful part of that experience was that I knew, deep in the center of my being, that I was a part of that woundedness. I was broken and incomplete. And so I began to sob.

Sobbing isn't the sort of thing a fourteen-year-old is supposed to do in front of peers. Particularly those of the female variety. Yet there I was, weeping myself snotty in the wake of a mystical experience.

My camp counselor noticed my tears. He took me aside and walked with me to an old aluminum canoe about fifteen yards from the campfire. The canoe hadn't been used in years and sat next to the nurse's cabin. As we sat in the canoe, he handed me a handkerchief, then asked me, "Would you like to accept Jesus as your Lord and Savior?"

I didn't know what that had to do with what I was experiencing, but I assumed he knew more about these sorts of things than I did. Between snotty sobs, I said yes. He then began to lead me through the "sinner's prayer."

As I look back, I regret saying yes. While I love Jesus and affirm the spiritual nature of that campfire experience, I don't believe what I was experiencing can be described as "being convicted of sin." It was something different—something that required discernment. However, the end result was that my deeply mystical experience was pushed and shaped into the easy template afforded by evangelicalism.

What I experienced was something of a conversion, but evangelicalism traditionally recognizes only one form of conversion. In subsequent years, when I returned to camp as a counselor, I was taught to see every crisis moment, every deep spiritual experience, as an opportunity for conversion.

Although the counselor was right to call me to repentance, he saw repentance narrowly as "saying you are sorry for sin and accepting Jesus as your personal Lord and Savior." I've come to understand it differently. Repentance is, unfortunately, often understood as an event rather than a posture. But when I say "repent" I mean to turn from one direction and to start walking in another. I mean that we need to start walking toward health and away from dis-health. My experience of suffering was, I believe, an invitation to engage the world differently. Such an invitation is the heart of repentance.

That wasn't the first time my experiences would be reshaped to fit within an evangelical paradigm. When I returned home from camp, the youth leader at the church I had just started attending gave me a Bible. He told me, "Start with the New Testament."

Because I was the socially awkward, book-reading type, it wasn't too much of a challenge for me to dive in and read the New Testament in a couple months. That isn't as much a testament to my intellectual aptitude as it is to my lack of social skills.

An interesting challenge quickly emerged. Because I was both fairly sophisticated as a reader (particularly in imaginative fiction) and unschooled in church superstitions, my intuitions quickly led me "astray." I assumed that the Bible was full of metaphors and poetry and prose and illustration. I didn't read it literally. Except for the parts where it was, you know, obvious. I treated the life and sermons of Jesus in a much more straightforward manner than, say, the book of Revelation or Jesus' parables.

Little did I realize that this was exactly backward. The really obvious statements about turning the other cheek or selling your possessions were obviously *not* obvious. And the seemingly obscure and esoteric visions found in Revelation were, in fact, pretty easy to understand. Just substitute "locusts" for "helicopters" and "beast with seven heads and ten horns" with "European Union."

I didn't grasp my backwardness right away. The first inkling came during youth Sunday school on a Sunday when later, during the service, we were going to honor the veterans. (Before I continue, it may be important for you to know that I was not, at this time, anything resembling a liberal. I was living in rural Minnesota. My family was fairly conservative. My father is a Vietnam War vet. I not only fished and hunted but had my own trapline when I was in elementary school. Nothing, environmentally speaking, could have contributed to what happened next.)

During Sunday school, the youth leader asked for prayer requests. And so, head filled with recently acquired New Testament insights of a radical Jesus, I offered to pray that God would forgive our church's war vets for killing their enemies.

That didn't go over very well. The youth leader got mad. Finger-pointing-in-face mad. I was genuinely confused by their anger. I wasn't trying to cause any trouble. I quickly learned that my way of reading the Gospels was inadequate and that my respect for my elders was insufficient.

I assumed that the mistake was on my part, so I *tried* to conform.

It took another year for the rest of my nascent radicalism to be extinguished. One occurrence stands out in my mind as the symbolic moment of that extinguishment.

I grew up near White Earth Reservation in Minnesota. Because of this, there was a higher concentration of poverty in my church than in most churches in the U.S. And, especially at that time in my life, I was poor.

And so, when one of the youth workers showed up to church with a brand-new, cherry-red Corvette, I reacted uncharitably. After all, the economic teachings of the New Testament are fairly consistent. I couldn't conceive of any justification for someone accruing such wealth when her brothers and sisters were experiencing relative poverty. And so, I rebuked her.

"Nice car, Wendy," I said sarcastically.

She replied, "Uh . . . thanks?"

"Probably cost a lot."

I could see the suspicion grow on her face as she responded, "It wasn't too bad."

"I bet you could have fed lots of hungry kids with the amount you spent on that car," I said smugly.

I chuckle as I think back on the argument that followed. My ethical insights were pretty good, considering how new I was to the whole

Christianity thing. But I had (and still have) an arrogant streak. Back then, I lacked tact. But what happened next was very much *not* funny.

Mine was a charismatic church. Not just the raise-your-hands-in-the-air kind; ours was the cast-out-demons kind. The youth leaders set up a special prayer time for me. During that two-hour session, they tried to cast the "Spirit of Poverty" out of me. They also prayed for my deliverance from other spirits like the "Spirit of Rebellion."

My radical instincts were cast out of me like devils.

That is how I became "Garth." With my fledgling radicalism exorcised, I began to see the Gospel as the animating force of the American Dream. God loved me and had a wonderful, America-shaped plan for my life. The Bible was a guidebook for good, clean living.

It was a decade before I revisited those themes that seemed, in the first year of my faith, to be central to the Gospel. It is odd: the things that were once considered demons I now consider central to my faith. And the things that were once central to my faith I now consider demonic. What was it that was cast out of me that day? And what was put in its place?

Garth no more. My son and I at an anti-fracking protest in 2012.
Jonas designed his own sign.

An Ode to Plastic Jesus

Entombed in plastic
My lord speaks
Brought low by thrifty men
His dangerous words forgotten
Divinity branded
His glory exchanged for a bar code
Cosmic Creator constrained
With a tiny TM
The Lion of Judah
Pushed into a cage
The Lamb of God
Sacrificed at the altar of "good taste"
The voice of the prophet
Silenced for profit
As affluence pours
Not to the poor
But to the affluent
In a sad twist Jesus sold at the table
Of the money changers
No one hears the cries
From inside his plastic tomb
As onward Christian soldiers
March to war
We dream an American Dream
Eyes shut to the Kingdom Vision
Followers of Jesus shopping in the city
With Jesus bound and gagged in the trunk
A day in the life of the Church
Of the American Empire

1

Exposing the Gospel of Empire

Among other works well pleasing to the Divine Majesty and cherished of our heart, this assuredly ranks highest, that in our times especially the Catholic faith and the Christian religion be exalted and be everywhere increased and spread, that the health of souls be cared for and that barbarous nations be overthrown and brought to the faith itself . . . We [the Papacy] command you [Spain] . . . to instruct the aforesaid inhabitants and residents and dwellers therein in the Catholic faith, and train them in good morals.

—Papal bull *Inter Caetera* (1493), issued by Pope Alexander VI

I GREW UP IN farm country. And where there are farmers, there are county fairs. In my early twenties, right after I got engaged (and toward the end of my "Garth" period), I was tricked into being an evangelist at the Becker County Fair.

Becker County takes its fair seriously, as I suspect is true in most farming areas. Becker County is also in the heart of the lakes country of Minnesota. Usually, the population of the county is about twenty thousand. But during the summer, with the influx of tourists, the population can triple.

So, with a steady flow of farmers, locals, and tourists, the fair was, as far as rural events go, a big deal.

One day my friend Joe, who is a pastor in those parts, invited me to the fair. I eagerly anticipated hot dogs, fried food, and the Tilt-A-Whirl.

But when we arrived, Joe turned to me and said, "Mark . . . I need a favor. I've got to do some errands, so I need you to work the booth."

"What booth?" I asked.

"The Heaven Booth," he replied. He had a smirk on his face.

The idea was simple: there was a booth with a big sign on the front that read, "Are you going to heaven when you die? Two-question test reveals answer!" Curious fairgoers would enter the booth, sit down, and be asked the following two questions:

1. Do you think you are going to heaven when you die?

2. Why?

Every single person who entered the booth answered question one in the affirmative. However, unless they answered the second question correctly (by explaining how Jesus died on the cross for their sins), I was supposed to break it to them that they were going to burn forever in hell. Thankfully, if they were interested, I would explain to them God's plan of salvation and help them find their way to heaven. Problem solved.

At that time in my life, I was committed to the practice of evangelism; I still assumed that the best thing anyone could do was to get as many people saved as possible—that was what Jesus put us here for. But I hated every minute of it. It felt so contrived . . . awkward . . . devoid of relationship. Nevertheless, that day I led several dozen people in praying a prayer to ask Jesus into their hearts.

Let me elaborate.

Early on in my shift, a beautiful young woman entered the Heaven Booth. She was wearing a crown and a sash. She was, presumably, Miss Becker County herself. Before she entered the booth, I was already feeling socially awkward. Cold-selling salvation to strangers isn't my idea of fun. When Miss Becker County entered the booth, the awkwardness became thick. Evangelizing strangers is one thing; evangelizing hot teenage strangers is another. I was overcome by a strange ambivalent blend of embarrassment, arousal, shame, and piety. I felt ashamed largely because I felt aroused and pious at the same time. And I felt embarrassed because I knew my face was red. Here I was, newly engaged and trying to lead people to

Jesus, and I was exercising nearly superhuman will to keep my eyes focused on Miss Becker County's face.

I don't exactly remember how she answered the two questions on the test. But I do remember that she failed. When I told her she was going to hell, she started to cry.

The only thing worse than a socially awkward twenty-year-old evangelizing an attractive beauty queen at a county fair Heaven Booth is a socially awkward twenty-year-old evangelizing a crying attractive beauty queen at a county fair Heaven Booth.

I couldn't look her in the eyes. And I was too self-conscious to look at her anywhere else. So I remember looking to the side and muttering something like "would you like to know how you can go to heaven when you die?"

Somewhere in the midst of a snotty sniffle, she said yes. So I proceeded to explain that God sent Jesus to die for her sins and that if she put her faith in him, she'd be saved. When we were done praying together, she looked at me with a huge smile.

"I've been going to church my whole life, and nobody ever did that for me before!" she said with genuine joy. She stood up and gave me a hug. At that moment, I wasn't thanking God for a won soul, I was thinking of her breasts. Which led to more feelings of embarrassment, arousal, shame, and (at least a little) piety.

Then she left.

I remember being relieved it was over.

But Miss Becker County returned . . . with every other pageant contestant. She was so filled with joy that she talked her colleagues into going to the Heaven Booth too. One by one, I awkwardly led a half-dozen beautiful young women to Jesus.

I never saw any of them again. The only record of my acquaintance with them was kept in my little evangelism notebook that I was asked to keep, recording a tally of souls saved.

I should have felt happy and proud that, on that summer day in the late nineties, several dozen fairgoers met their Lord because of me. But the experience left me feeling confused and a little ashamed. They were little more than numbers to me that day. I objectified them all—not just the young ladies who left me feeling impious. Is there any great difference between a young man who keeps a tally on his bedpost and one who keeps a tally in his Bible cover? Both render something deeply intimate into a transaction. Both turn people into numbers. Both turn people into objects of conquest.

Much of what passes for the propagation of the gospel is actually acts of oppression. When the saving of souls is of ultimate value, it can become easy for other values to be pushed aside. This evangelistic impulse turns every mystical experience into an altar call and every person into a soul to be saved. And, historically, Christians have shown an ability to care for someone's soul while dismissing their bodies, their land, or their dignity.

To many of those who have experienced oppression in the name of Jesus, Christianity has been about conquest, subduing creation, asserting its superiority over other faiths, and creating a mechanism for alleviating the guilt for such unethical behavior.

Somewhere along the way, Christianity gave way to Christendom—the establishment of Christianity as a dominant cultural force. Christendom was built through means that dishonor Christ. Almost everyone acknowledges this today. Few celebrate the gains of the Crusades, the Inquisition, or the conquest of the so-called New World (with its subjugation of indigenous peoples and its reliance upon slave labor); each of these was carried out to secure and expand Christendom. While most Christians easily recognize the sins of the past, they rarely, if ever, see how such misdeeds have any connection to our Christianity today. Usually, our response to past injustices is to suggest that they have nothing to do with "real" Christianity. Christianity, therefore, remains pristine. It goes without saying that, could we use a gigantic time machine to transport all of today's Christians to the Crusades or the Inquisition or the conquest of the New World or to the early days of American slavery, then such atrocities would never have happened.

As we continue our march into the future, we believe that we have become better people with better societies. Perhaps we are as blind to our own complicity in injustice as the Christians of the past. One of the bad habits of Western Christianity is that it affirms the Myth of Progress—that the continual march of our civilization toward a better world is inevitable. It is easy to believe that the devils of our human nature live in the past—that we must simply stay the course and the world will get better, even if sociopolitical, environmental, economic, and spiritual evidence suggests otherwise. This naïve optimism serves to justify the sins of the past and keeps us from pursuing justice in the present.

If we want to see our past and our present with open eyes, we need to remove the blinders of self-justification. What if, to help us see our faith with new eyes, we granted the oppressed the right to define Christianity? What if, that day at the Heaven Booth, I had asked the beauty contestants what they thought made a person a Christian? Perhaps it would have challenged me to be more like Christ. Perhaps asking such questions at the macro level would help us learn why Christianity has been enmeshed in some of the most egregious examples of oppression in our world.

For two thousand years, various forms of insidious supremacy (whether it is white supremacy, national supremacy, or class supremacy) have been tied with Christian supremacy. "Christian supremacy" is the idea that Christianity is superior to all other religions and, by extension, Christians are superior to non-Christians. When pushed even further, it is the belief that Christian culture and political structures should, in some way, dominate. Because Christ is sovereign, those who most represent Christ can be sovereign. The idea of the "supremacy of Christ" has been used to justify war, economic exploitation, and genocide.

CHRISTIANITY IS CONQUEST

In 2010, I interviewed Dakota scholar Waziyatawin for the Iconcast podcast. It was a painful interview. In it she suggested that there is little hope that Christianity will have a place in creating a just world because Christianity, at its core, is about subduing the land, asserting its dominance over people of other faiths, and establishing itself as the one true religion.

Until that conversation, I had found it easy to argue against such logic. After all, I reasoned, that isn't what *real* Christianity is about. But in that moment, I knew that it was not my place to argue. The Dakota were subjugated in the name of Christ. If the best proof I have of the goodness of Christianity is nice ideals, then my proof is worthless. Christianity is proven by deeds (isn't that what the book of James teaches?).

Waziyatawin isn't alone in believing that Christianity has no place in creating a just world because Christianity, in the experience of so many, is about subduing the land, asserting its superiority over people of other faiths, and assuming the role of the world's only true religion.

These qualities, if indeed central to Christianity, make it the ideal imperial religion. I'm sure that more than a handful of Roman emperors, European rulers, and American presidents would agree.

The argument that Christianity is intrinsically oppressive is nothing new, but it persists. I believe that the dominant form of Christianity, as understood by the majority of Christians throughout the ages, is inherently oppressive and will inevitably lead to Empire. There are, of course, expressions of Christianity that resist imperialism. But a Christianity that is willing to use the Sword will *always* nurture Empire.

At this point I should pause to explain what I mean when I use the word *empire*. Political scientists would likely define empire as what happens when one nation dominates others so that it can exploit subjugated peoples and extract the resources of subjugated lands. One people group or nation dominates other groups or nations through political, economic, and military means.

In the past, empire-building was rather blatant. Today, it is debated whether or not the United States functions as an empire. My own view is that with well over seven hundred military bases around the world, vast territory, economic dominance, and two military occupations, it isn't a difficult case to make.

Others, however, argue that Empire works differently in our postcolonial age. Since the mid-twentieth century, the political machines of control have been increasingly replaced with economic controls. For example, there is no need for the United States to have direct control over subordinate nations. Everyone can vote and still end up being dominated. As long as the people of the world are dependent upon our modern global economy, they remain under control without the need for military conflict. Military force is reserved for those who do not remain dependent on our economic system (regardless of their political system). Our modern experience of globalization offers a subtle form of imperialism: nations may seem to exercise their own sovereignty, but the ones who shape economic realities also shape global destinies. The global economy, the destinies of millions of the world's poor, and the resources of lands around the world are controlled by a global elite who, more than anywhere else, find their center of power in the United States of America.

But it isn't the logistical workings of Empire that I want to focus on. Rather, I want to focus on the ethos of Empire—how does an empire understand and justify itself? And how does the logic of Empire (which is about security, domination, and control) become intertwined with Christianity?

Our proximity to power and affluence gives us a strange perspective from which to read the gospel. The logic of Empire is the expeditious, organized pursuit of security, prosperity, and control; and the best way to ensure these things is through domination. Our entire way of life depends upon this pursuit. Yet it is contrary to the life and teachings of Jesus, who foreswore security as he walked among the marginalized and challenged the civil and religious authorities; who offered people freedom and confronted those who sought to control others; who upheld and loved the weak rather than dominate them. We find ourselves trying to justify our way of life while worshiping One who challenges our way of life.

When the way of Jesus came into direct confrontation with imperial logic, the political and religious leaders conspired to kill him. And when Jesus' death didn't kill the movement, the empire found itself with a small but growing radically anti-imperial movement. The early Christians were hated by the powerful.

But things change. While it can be argued that the growth of Christianity had a positive impact on the Roman Empire, I do not believe that the inverse is true. As Christianity grew in influence, it became politically advantageous to "play nice" with Christianity. Rodney Stark suggests that in the fifty-year period between 250 and the dawn of the fourth century, Christianity grew from just over one million to more than six million (out of a total population of sixty million). In other words, within about a generation, the Christian population increased from a little over 1 percent to 10 percent of the population. Within another generation, Christians would total more than half of the Roman Empire.[1] By the time the emperor Constantine came to power in 306, Christianity was a major force in Roman society.

As Christianity gained respectfulness in the empire, its more radical tenets were downplayed. Traditionally, Constantine is blamed for this shift, and for some good reasons. If you are the most powerful military leader in the history of the world, controlling vast territory and wealth, it is hard to embrace the radical teachings of Jesus. You can't fuel an empire with love of enemies. If you are trying to subjugate the world, the Sermon on the Mount makes bad foreign policy.

But the shift began before Constantine. H. A. Drake argues that as bishops grew in wealth and influence in the decades before Constantine, they grew in political power.[2] Christianity was already becoming corrupt before it was in bed with the emperor.

Traditional readings of Genesis (about subduing the land) mixed with traditional views of the Lordship of Christ (giving his followers

1. Stark, *Rise of Christianity*, 6–7.
2. Drake, *Constantine and the Bishops*.

socioreligious superiority) mixed with the evangelistic impulse of the Great Commission (giving us a mandate to extend Christ's rule to the ends of the earth) are problematic enough as they stand. But if you add the willingness to use violence to accomplish these ends, you create the perfect empire cocktail. Before the imperial legitimization of Christianity, violence was largely rejected. There were rare examples of Christian soldiers before the time of Constantine, but the first known reference wasn't until AD 173, where Christian soldiers belonged to *Legio XII Fulminata*. Afterward, the use of violence became increasingly seen as a viable way of enforcing orthodoxy.[3] A Christianity that is willing to use the Sword will *always* nurture Empire. If you *weaponize* the teachings of Jesus, they become imperial.

THE SUBJUGATION OF CREATION

Genesis 1:28 says, "God blessed them and said to them, 'Be fruitful and increase in number; fill the earth and subdue it. Rule over the fish of the sea and the birds of the air and over every living creature that moves on the ground.'" Traditionally, the Christian understanding of creation sets the human being apart from nature, advocates human control of nature, and implies that the natural world was created solely for our use. It continues, in the minds of many within Judeo-Christian traditions, to justify (or even compel) our deep exploitation of the earth in the name of advancing civilization. As Richard Bauckham, professor of New Testament studies at the University of St. Andrews, writes, "The idea of human dominion has been the ideological justification of human domination and exploitation of nature."[4]

Genesis 1–2 has been used, more than any other passage in Scripture, to justify the exploitation of resources required to make Empire possible. Empires require the sort of surplus and hoarding that one cannot achieve through a simple harmonious relationship with the earth; the amount of food and natural resources required to fuel armies necessitates that everyone in a society take more than they need to support an ever-expanding force. This was true of the Roman Empire and it is true today. Empire requires exploitation of the land.

In recent decades, Christians have embraced a model of stewardship that moves beyond themes of domination and exploitation. However, as Richard Bauckham suggests, "While stewardship avoids the themes of

3. Gaddis, *There Is No Crime.*

4. Bauckham, *Bible and Ecology*, 37.

domination, exploitation, and re-creation that fuelled the modern project, it retains the purely vertical relationship . . . It is a limitation that suggests that the stewardship model by itself could be a perilously one-sided model for a relationship so complex as the human relationship to other creatures."[5]

As long as we see our relationship with creation in such a vertical manner, exploitation is likely to continue. As long as our needs are placed hierarchically above the needs of creation, our need to secure and safeguard ourselves in an environmentally fragile world will continue to fuel unfettered consumption of resources. We need to learn how to practice mutual submission with creation as fellow creatures.

So, while our rhetoric has shifted toward a more environmentally "aware" idea of stewardship, we continue to use the earth's resources with a primary concern for our own amusement. For example, although more in our society have come to embrace "green capitalism"—attempting to replace everyday consumer goods with earth-friendly alternatives—there has been no slowdown in consumption overall. We are willing, when we can afford it, to use special light bulbs and buy biodegradable dish soap. But are we willing to radically simplify our lives? Few environmental scientists believe these small gestures are enough. For many Christians, the exploitation of the earth is justifiable; it is, after all, in our job description.

Historically, when a people group expands in order to subdue the land, it is willing to subdue "lesser" peoples as peasant labor for agriculture and industry. While the scriptural mandate itself doesn't justify the exploitation of "lesser" nations or peoples, historian David Armitage argues that, at least within the British Empire, "God's commands to replenish the earth and assert dominion over it provided a superior right to possession for those who cultivated the land more productively than others."[6] If we embrace the subjugation of land as a divine mandate, then those who subjugate "better" have a better claim upon the land.

However, to be fair, the colonizers were probably well intentioned. Their desire was, after all, to make the subjugated more like the subjugators—which is an attempt at coerced equality—call it "compassionate conquest." And the compassionate conquerors benefited as well, since they were the ones who knew how to cultivate the land to its potential. Everyone wins!

We may recoil at this logic and recognize the dark stain it has left in the history of Western civilization. However, I believe a version of this

5. Bauckham, *Bible and Ecology*, 28.

6. Armitage, *British Empire*, 97.

logic remains prevalent in our society. For example, I know a man who paid thousands of dollars for land in Central America—land that had recently been purchased from indigenous people for mere hundreds. When I challenged the man on the justice of such transactions, he replied, "Those people wouldn't know what to do with all of that money!" I have talked with many people who justify the relative poverty of the "rest of the world" because they suppose it to be not only less economically developed than the so-called First World but also less developed in most ways. How far is this from the old logic of domination?

In our day, we see economic exploitation and military conquest offered in the name of "spreading democracy" or "Third World development." The assumption then (and now) is that it is better for "them" to become like "us."

I have no doubt that most modern exploitation is fueled by good intentions. Many assume that capitalism and democracy can nurture prosperity and freedom. The truth falls far short of good intentions. Modern corporations—the ones that meet most of our wants and needs—go to the ends of the earth to secure natural resources for the betterment of First World people at the expense of locals. Look at the label of your shirt and ask, "Would I be willing to live like the man, woman, or child who sewed this shirt?"

While modern economic exploitation is (usually) done legally, the system intrinsically disadvantages the locals. It is the powerful that set the rules, after all. Corporations can help shape the very laws they observe, even if the result is exploitation and oppression of locals. This leads to the ridiculous situation of local workers being paid mere dollars a day and a small profit from the sale of extracted resources; meanwhile, First World people are able to gain relatively cheap goods while enjoying a comfortable standard of living.

This sort of behavior is simply a continuation of a pattern that was set by earlier Christian imperialism and colonialism. While the folks at Halliburton (one of the largest extractors of oil and natural gas in the world) probably don't quote the Scriptures to justify their exploitation of natural resources and local populations, it seems that centuries of misreading Genesis 1 have made it possible for "good Christian folk" to support such activities as part of our larger mandate to use the world for our own purposes.

Is this the message of Genesis 1:28? Are we the Lords of the Earth whose divine mandate is to bring creation into subjugation? Can we assume that within the early verses of Genesis, God grants us the right to farm, mine, and build across the face of the earth as we see fit?

It is a mistake to assume that Genesis mandates our role as benevolent dictators of the earth. As Ched Myers points out,

> Another wordplay associates the summons to "multiply" (*rabah*) and to "rule" (*radah*) . . . The primary task was to conserve the fertility of the land for the next generation—not to plunder it for short-term gain. Yet because the early Israelites were eking out a living on marginal and drought-plagued land, this task often felt like a wrestling match with the elements. It is in this sense that we should interpret the phrase "fill the land and subdue it," which has fueled modern theologies of domination.[7]

Since there is a reasonably non-imperial and non-exploitative way of reading Genesis 1, it is worth asking, Why is the conventional reading so top-down? Do we believe in the human dominion of creation because it is what Scripture teaches? Or do we interpret Scripture as teaching dominion because it serves imperial interests to read it that way?

THE SUBJUGATION OF THE NATIONS

> God exalted him to the highest place and gave him the name that is above every name, that at the name of Jesus every knee should bow, in heaven and on earth and under the earth, and every tongue confess that Jesus Christ is Lord, to the glory of God the Father. (Phil 2:9b–11)

It isn't that hard to make the leap from "my God is better than your God" to "my group is better than your group" and then to "my group should dominate your group." However, just because you believe in the supremacy of Christ, it doesn't *automatically* mean that you're going to dominate non-Christian groups (or groups that aren't following Christ in the best way). Or does it? If you believe that you are in the "in" group and that all others are going to hell, isn't it at least *more* likely that you'll dominate them?

The basic structures of Christianity (with some clear exceptions) make for an excellent imperial religion—you have a single God who demands that all worship him and him alone. You have a common creed. You have one church. A unified religion brought in line with a unified government is an elegant way to control the peoples. All that remains is to theologize away Jesus' ethical teachings.

7. Myers, "To Serve and Preserve."

Jesus calls us give to the poor rather than saving up for ourselves. Jesus teaches us to love our enemies, not to bomb them to "stabilize the region." Jesus taught us to practice forgiveness, not to pursue vengeance. Jesus taught us to practice hospitality to strangers, not to live in fear of them. Jesus welcomed us into a new way of loving each other like family, which does away with elevating some over others.

Once notions of Jesus' care for the marginalized and his insistence on enemy-love are swept aside, it becomes easier to imagine a world in which Church and Empire work in tandem to suppress non-Christian peoples in order to (1) assert the sovereignty of Christ over false gods and (2) establish Christian civilization over pagan tribes.

The superiority of Christianity over other religions has given Western imperialism the sheen of altruism for almost two thousand years. Another facet of compassionate conquest is offering the conquered a superior religion. What is temporal subjugation compared to the gift of eternal life?

It is usually assumed that religious motivation for conquest is a thing of the past—at least in the West. We take comfort that such a mindset is no longer with us . . . or is it? As I mentioned earlier, it is "democracy" rather than "Christianity" that is often articulated as the driving force of our imperialistic actions. Exceptionalism—the idea that one nation, like the United States, stands above other nations as a beacon of hope, freedom, and goodness and has a unique responsibility to urge the world toward hope, freedom, and goodness—is what drives imperialism. If a nation's interests trump the interests of other nations, then it is easier to justify the subjugation of other nations.

One cannot justify Empire without somehow believing that one's own nation is superior to other nations. We justify our imperialism with our exceptionalism. How much is this superiority complex rooted in some sort of Christian exceptionalism?

I don't think our broadly Christian roots are incidental to our imperialism; they are central. The engine of Western imperialism is the quasi-Christian set of national myths that deceive us into believing that we alone embody the good life and should spread that life to the rest of the world. The American Dream is our Gospel.

I will delve deeper into the relationship between imperialism and mythology later. However, it may be helpful to briefly explain the way in which the American Dream functions as a powerful imperial myth. It is so deeply assumed in our society that middle-class existence (homeownership, college education, marriage that produces children, car ownership, disposable income, etc.) is the Good Life. Christianity largely exists in our society to nourish this Good Life. It is such a Good Life that almost any act is justifiable if it either (*a*) secures that Good Life for us or (*b*) promotes that Good Life among other peoples—particularly our enemies. The American Dream is so deeply entrenched that it is largely unquestioned.

America serves as a brilliant example of using Christianity to reinforce Empire. If we see the Roman emperors (like Constantine) utilizing Christianity to strengthen their empire, then it is no less true of the American Empire. Empires require myths that captivate the imaginations of its subjects. Without powerful myths in place, people will see that the emperor has no clothes. And, for better or worse, the American civil religion is perhaps the crowning achievement of Christian imperialism.

It is undeniable that our conquest of North America (and the conquest of the New World in general) was predicated upon Christian religious superiority. Pope Alexander VI agreed. That's why, in *Inter Caetera*, he divvies up Latin America between Spain and Portugal, justifying himself with these words:

> Among other works well pleasing to the Divine Majesty and cherished of our heart, this assuredly ranks highest, that in our times especially the Catholic faith and the Christian religion be exalted and be everywhere increased and spread, that the health of souls be cared for and that barbarous nations be overthrown and brought to the faith itself . . . We [the papacy] command you [Spain] . . . to instruct the aforesaid inhabitants and residents and dwellers therein in the Catholic faith, and train them in good morals.

Such logic was repeatedly employed to justify the US conquest of North America as well (which was, after all, our Manifest Destiny). Read these words of Andrew Jackson:

> The removal of the Indians beyond the limits and jurisdiction of the states does not place them beyond the reach of philanthropic aid and Christian instruction. On the contrary, those whom philanthropy or religion may induce to live among them in their new abode will be more free in the exercise of their benevolent functions than if they had remained within the limits of the states, embarrassed by their internal regulations. Now subject to no control but the superintending agency of the general government, exercised with the sole view of preserving peace, they may proceed unmolested in the interesting experiment of gradually advancing a

community of American Indians from barbarism to the habits and enjoyments of civilized life.[8]

At this point, you may be asking, "So what, Mark? It isn't Christianity's fault that America or Britain or Rome used the supremacy of Christ to legitimize Empire!" Ah, but the Christianity so many of us have inherited comes to us from America or Britain or Rome. For most of us, Christianity cannot be separated from its imperial roots. Christianity isn't a set of disembodied ideas—we *learn* Christianity. And, for most of the world, Christianity is an inheritance enmeshed with imperialistic sentiments.

If we are to challenge imperialism, we must not only try to disarm the deadly idea that the supremacy of Christ legitimizes the supremacy of Christians. We must also, I believe, disarm the idea of Christ's supremacy. And we must learn from those movements and traditions within Christianity that have rejected different forms of domination.

In Philippians, Paul describes the nature of Jesus' rulership: "Who, though he was in the form of God, did not regard equality with God as something to be exploited, but emptied himself, taking the form of a slave" (2:6–7a). Jesus' "rule" is inextricably tied to his humility and servanthood.

This isn't to say that Jesus is a benevolent tyrant, that the posture of his reign is humble. Rather, the very nature of his reign is humble. Roger Haydon Mitchell calls this form of rule "kenarchy," the composite of the Greek words *keno* ("to empty") and *archo* ("to rule"). Mitchell writes, "Kenarchy . . . proposes that the behavior of self-emptying love . . . is the fullness of divine rule."[9] Jesus' reign isn't merely humble; he reigns through humility.

So, instead of thinking of Christianity as a superior religion, wouldn't it be better to assert Christianity's inferiority? What if Christians everywhere had assumed that they should take the humble jobs instead of trying to influence Empire by seeking high position? The entire notion of the "supremacy" or "sovereignty" of Christ is misguided (at least if taken in a straightforward manner). Imperial language in the New Testament is largely ironic—or, at the very least, redefined. To say "Jesus is Lord" is to assert that Caesar is not. And if Jesus' Lordship is defined by its intrinsic humility, then what does it now mean? When we port conventional definitions for those ideas into Christ and the church, we're bound to end up in the kind of mess we find ourselves in today.

8. Jackson, "Third Annual Message," December 6, 1831. Quoted in Williams, *Addresses and Messages of the Presidents*, 2:763.

9. Mitchell, *Church, Gospel, and Empire*, 174.

EVANGELISM AND CONQUEST

> He said to them, "Go into all the world and preach the good news
> to all creation. Whoever believes and is baptized will be saved, but
> whoever does not believe will be condemned." (Mark 16:15–16)

For a majority of people throughout the ages, Christianity has been a religion of Empire. It has legitimized the exploitation of creation and the
subjugation of peoples. A gospel that was meant to challenge Empire has
become the gospel *of* Empire.

So, when we speak of "evangelism" today, we are likely speaking of
an imperial evangelism. Evangelism (and its well-traveled brother, "missions") has been a vehicle for imperialism. This trend continues. Even the
most "contextual" of ministries will often carry imperialistic thinking.
Most Americans (and I assume this is true for most Westerners) are familiar enough with their own cultural embeddedness to question how much
they've adapted their understanding of their faith (to varying extents). But
most Christians I know aren't as willing or able to challenge their embedded imperial context or examine their own power. It is acceptable to talk
about cultural relevance in ministry, but seldom do we speak, with honesty,
of cultural power.

And so, missionaries continue to go to the ends of the earth with an
understanding of the Gospel that was shaped by a successive chain of imperial contexts. And, for the most part, Christianity conformed to those
contexts.

Certainly, there were always pioneers who went to the ends of the
earth with a message of love and mutuality. Not all of these missionaries
were so deeply imperialistic in their thinking that they unquestioningly
supported their empires. Quite the contrary.

There have always been prophetic voices like Bartolomé de las Casas
who spoke out against oppression (mostly). But they were a small part of a
larger apparatus of oppression. And rarely, if ever, were such men willing
to be traitors for the cause of Christ; they spoke challenging words against
oppression, but only to a point. When it came to the conquest and colonization of the "New World," the Vatican was entirely complicit—and the
church as a whole followed its lead. While the church did seem to affirm
the humanity of the natives, it was generally assumed that such natives
should submit to Christian rule. To its credit, I suppose, the church's voice
called for a softening of the harsher atrocities of conquest. However, it is

difficult to imagine that such conquest would have happened at all without Christendom.

But you, the reader, have heard all of this before. It is ancient history. Why don't we just move on? Because we haven't repented of our Gospel, and as a result, we still tell the same sort of Gospel. Christianity is still imperial.

Today, when missionaries go to foreign lands, they are certainly more progressive. But, generally speaking, missionaries have joined the values of modern "democracy" with their understanding of the Gospel. We no longer embrace the ancient understanding of evangelism as powerlessness:

> After this the Lord appointed seventy-two others and sent them two by two ahead of him to every town and place where he was about to go. He told them, "The harvest is plentiful, but the workers are few. Ask the Lord of the harvest, therefore, to send out workers into his harvest field. Go! I am sending you out like lambs among wolves. Do not take a purse or bag or sandals; and do not greet anyone on the road." (Luke 10:1–4)

Conservatives tend to bring a conformist Gospel filtered through centuries of Christendom. Liberals tend to bring a social Gospel that makes folks dependent upon the generosity of imperial citizens. In both cases, there is an often unrecognized power differential. It is one thing for the powerless to evangelize the powerful (read Acts). It is another thing altogether for the powerful to evangelize the relatively powerless.

This leads to all sorts of strange modern-day manifestations of the evangelism of Empire. In the eighties, there were reports of Wycliffe Bible translators involved in funneling information to the CIA, which led to the martyrdom of Óscar Romero, Ignacio Ellacuría, and others.[10] Christian missionaries contributed to the destabilization of regions, making them more susceptible to Western interventionism. In recent years, journalists have exposed the shady activities of some within YWAM—the world's largest missions organization—trying to influence foreign governments as well as being linked to an organization called "the Family." The Family is a conservative religious organization that started the National Prayer Breakfast and has incredible access to US politicians.[11]

If you think about it, there is a sort of warped logic to imperial evangelism. If the Gospel of Jesus is "repent, for the Kingdom is near," then the Gospel of Empire is "repent, for the Empire is at your borders." We have

10. See Colby and Dennett, *Thy Will Be Done.*
11. Sharlet, *C Street.*

replaced a Gospel of liberation with one of enslavement. We have substituted the gifts of the Spirit for consumer capitalism and mutual submission for free-market democracy.

Global evangelism often serves to prepare nations for foreign interventionism. This is true of conservative groups who link US influence with the cause of Christ, as well as progressive groups that see people of the "developing world" as objects of charity rather than the subjects of their own liberation.

To both the conservative and the progressive citizens of Empire, the tendency is to bring a good news to those who lack and to see the citizens of Empire as the liberator. This continues the old lie. Why is it that so many teenage missionaries are sent to Mexico? It is because, by both conservative and liberal Christian measures, Mexicans "lack." And the more our missionaries go to such places, the more they are captivated by the imagination of Empire.

Even now, in an age heralded as "post-Christian" or at least "post-Christendom," the logic of imperial Christianity lingers even in the most secular places. The content of the message may have changed, but the medium is still the strange messianic imperialism passed down by the Romans. And our faith is still being shaped, even as Christian institutions lose influence, by imperial logic.

CHAPTER ONE GROUP GUIDE

 Summary

Christianity, in its most dominant expressions, has not only become a tool of Empire, but has provided its mythological core. We've inherited an understanding of the Gospel that legitimizes the conquest and subjugation of peoples and land. And we've understood this as an almost altruistic act. Even as our society shifts toward post-Christendom, the myths basically stay the same. We've merely substituted the word "democracy" for "Gospel" to continue our well-intentioned subjugation.

 Discussion Questions

1. In what ways is the author's experience with Christianity like your own? How is it different?

2. How do you see imperial Christianity being practiced in the world today?

3. How do you feel about the author's suggestion that we embrace the *inferiority* of Christianity?

✘ Group Practice

- Give people a few minutes to page through the Gospels (if they don't have a hard copy, they could pull it up on their phone, and if they don't have a smartphone, they can spend that time in inner reflection). Then, on a large piece of paper, write down all the things that Jesus seems most passionate about.

- Give participants a few minutes to look over a newspaper or magazine (hard copy or phone is okay) or spend time in recollection of the most pressing news or pop-cultural events of the past couple of months. Then, on a large piece of paper, write down all the things that our society seems most passionate about. Save these sheets of paper for your discussion of chapter 5.

- What are some points of agreement? What are some points of difference?

🕯 Close with a time of silence or prayer.

🎓 Suggested Resources

An Indigenous Peoples' History of the United States, by Roxanne Dunbar-Ortiz
Living in the Shadow of the Cross, by Paul Kivel
Manifest Destiny: American Expansion and the Empire of Right, by Anders Stephanson
The Doctrine of Discovery: Unmasking the Domination Code (documentary)
The Mission (film)

GOD IS NOT FOUND

god is not found
in pure things
but in cracks and smudges
that cry for healing

god is not found
in big ideas
but in the small space
between two people

god is not found
in the stories that build worlds
but in the little truths
that tear them down

2

Unveiling the Myths We Live By

Mundus vult decipi, ergo decipiatur.
"The world wants to be deceived, so let it be deceived."

—PETRONIUS, FIRST CENTURY CE

IT IS BAD ENOUGH that our Christianity has fueled imperialism. If the story ended there, we could simply stop contributing to the imperial machine and fix things. Christianity not only injected some of its DNA into Empire (thus Christianizing it), but Empire has injected its DNA into Christianity, thus imperializing our Christianity. It is nearly impossible to understand how deep the infection goes.

Ours is a faith that has, for the most part, worked in opposition to its object. Christendom has, in its imperial journey, cast out much of its anti-imperial core like demons.

Certainly, there are exceptions. But they stand out as exceptions because of their rarity. There are many saints who challenged the growing imperial tendencies of our faith: St. Francis, Martin Luther King Jr., Dorothy Day, Óscar Romero . . . the list goes on. But they were in the margins. Theirs were mustard seeds of faith standing against a growing mountain of unfaith. And I still believe that such faith will cast that mountain into the sea.

THE PRINCIPALITIES AND POWERS

The New Testament has a strange way of talking about imperial realities. When the book of Revelation explores the reality of imperialism, it offers apocalyptic imagery of beasts with horns and prostitutes riding dragons—things better suited for Led Zeppelin album covers than serious conversation about modern global problems. The Apostle Paul uses language like "the principalities and powers" to express imperial realities.[1]

It is easy to assume that things like "principalities and powers" are either imaginary or disembodied spiritual realities, whereas things like empires and nations are real and tangible. But to Paul, these were closely linked realities. In fact, he uses the same words to describe both human structures of authority and demonic realities.[2]

The principalities and powers are social structures—social realities—that "manage" humanity. Whenever we find ourselves relating to one another, our Creator, or our environment in a way that is abstracted or indirect or prescribed, it is usually the result of our participation with the principalities and powers.

In order to understand the nature of principalities and powers, we need to explore the nature of abstraction. Abstraction is the process by which ideas are distanced from objects. In other words, abstraction happens when we talk about the idea of people not the concrete reality that is the person in front of you. Abstraction creates layers of distance between things and people. And in some ways, this is very useful. Some might say this is essential to being human.

Abstraction helps us step back to understand the patterns at work in our world that can't be explained by looking at things directly. For example,

---

1. There are a number of great resources that explore the shape of the principalities and powers, their relationship with the demonic, and their role in imperial myths. The classics for this are William Stringfellow's *Ethic for Christians and Other Aliens in a Strange Land*, Walter Wink's *Engaging the Powers*, René Girard's *I See Satan Fall Like Lightning*, and Jacques Ellul's *New Demons*.

2. John Howard Yoder is one of a number of scholars who make this case. In *The Politics of Jesus* he argues, "Something of the same stimulating confusion is present in the thought of the apostle Paul as he applies some of the same thought patterns to different challenges in different contexts. He speaks of 'principalities and powers,' and of 'thrones and dominions,' thus using language of political color. But he can also use cosmological language like 'angels and archangels,' 'elements,' 'heights and depths.' Or the language can be religious: 'law,' 'knowledge.' Sometimes the reader perceives a parallelism in all these concepts, sometimes not" (137).

it is helpful to explore poverty as an abstraction as a way of understanding the forces that may cause a person's material suffering. However, we run into problems if our imaginations remain abstracted.

Religion is itself an abstraction. When animated by love, religion allows us to reflect upon our relationship with God, with our neighbor, and with the world so that we can grow deeper in our love. But religion is as likely to obscure our experience of God as to illuminate it. We can get wrapped up in beliefs and ideas and, somehow, remain aloof from the things those beliefs and ideas point toward. We can care about poverty but not the poor woman on the corner. We can care about the idea of love but leave it fundamentally unexpressed.

Abstraction begets evil. This is one of the assumptions I bring to the writing of this book. Abstraction keeps us from experiencing things directly. It allows us to lose individual human beings or trees or lakes or a flower in the midst of concepts like "humanity" or "nature." By abstracting war, the nightly news makes it feel like the same sort of thing as weather or sports. By abstracting complex realities of suffering and struggle, we can feel disconnected from those realities yet still somehow knowledgeable about them. There is some benefit to this—it can allow us to consider perspectives other than our own, thus helping us grow in wisdom and compassion.

Principalities and powers need abstraction to survive. And, in turn, principalities and powers keep us "stuck" in abstracted thinking so that real relationships serve the purposes of the principalities and powers. The powers and principalities work to keep us separated and alienated from one another. No wonder that when the Apostle Paul tried to name "the enemy" of the Gospel, he mentioned not only Satan but also these things called "principalities and powers."[3]

The only way to get otherwise good people to accept a world of war and exploitation and greed is to mire them in an abstracted way of thinking, where such things are simply "the way things are."

Where I grew up, we usually thought of these "things" as generals in satanic armies. They had territories—like the Principality of Minnesota or the Principality of Hoboken. But reality is much more complex (and immediate) than that.

The powers aren't born in hell. They are born in the common spaces of our humanity—in the brokenness of our communities, families, and

3. See Eph 6.

relationships. They aren't born out of hate but out of lack. They are born not out of cruelty but out of incomplete love.

Scripture tells us that they are created by God (Col 1:15–17). They started out as a creative expression of God, serving divine purposes. But they are fallen. All too easily, wickedness creeps in. Greed seeps in and creates structures of economic oppression. Rage creeps in, and scapegoats become victimized. Structures and ideas and systems created to help us live in harmony with one another, God, and creation have become an enemy of God and creation.

The powers grow in the distance that exists between God, people, and the land. They are usually born to fill in the gaps: to help us reach one another and be united. But, in their fallenness, they fail to bring us closer to one another. Instead, they exist as layers of abstraction between us. Over time, structures meant to bring us closer to God (like formal prayer, the Eucharist, Scripture, etc.) can harden and end up actually keeping people from God. Things meant to bring people together (like families) can become abusive and alienating. And structures meant to help us live in harmony with the rest of creation (like tools) can harm creation and render us unable to relate to it healthfully. This is the sad nature of the powers. They usually spring up to help us relate to each other better, but become instruments of oppression.

Over time, the principalities and powers become assumed—they become uncontested parts of the fabric of reality. We cannot imagine spirituality apart from institutional religion. It seems impossible for humans to live together without things like nations. We don't know how to survive without going to the grocery store to buy things that were shipped to us from a place far away. These things are treated like necessities, yet human beings throughout history have lived without them. We no longer recognize them as abstractions. We have forgotten how to relate to God, other human beings, and the land without these abstractions.

An empire is a nexus of principalities and powers—a center of massive spiritual collusion where such principalities and powers work together to serve Satan, the prince of the "world" (see Luke 4:5–7; 2 Cor 4:4). Walter Wink compellingly argues that the word *cosmos*—which is often translated "world" in the New Testament—should perhaps be conceived as a "domination system." In other words, the "world" being referred to in the New Testament isn't the dirt and grass and flowers beneath our feet. It isn't nature. Rather, it is the social constructs that take place on top of that dirt—society and buildings and human interactivity.

Few human beings will willingly prefer the way of subjugation to the way of liberation. Few choose death over life. So why is it that so many participate in systems antithetical to their stated values? Much of this may be attributed to weakness or selfishness, but not all.

Sometimes folks go along with systems of death because they are forced to. But I suspect most of us in the West do so because we are clueless. This difference—between folks who participate in systems of death through coercion versus those who do so through clueless willingness—is sometimes presented as the "*1984* versus *Brave New World*" systems of control.

Brave New World was written by Aldous Huxley in 1931; *1984* was written by George Orwell in 1949. Orwell and Huxley were contemporaries. They were both Englishmen. And they were both fairly progressive. While they may have agreed on what constitutes a good society, they had different concerns about social control in the modern world.

In *1984* folks are controlled overtly. The evil system of *1984* is like a stereotype of the Soviet Union, which reflects Orwell's staunch anti-Stalinist thinking. Folks know that they are being controlled but feel powerless to change their fate.

In *Brave New World*, folks go along with systemic evil because they are distracted by entertainment and pleasure. They are granted so many choices that they mistake choice for autonomy; they fail to notice how thoroughly they are controlled.

The evil system of *Brave New World* is like a stereotype of the United States. When folks can visit whatever websites they want, eat whatever foods they want, and watch whatever movies they want, they don't notice the injustices that happen around the world, nor do they realize that the most importance choices may not be theirs to make.

In the foreword to his classic work *Amusing Ourselves to Death*, Neil Postman comments on the differences between Huxley's and Orwell's dystopian visions:

> Orwell feared that the truth would be concealed from us. Huxley feared the truth would be drowned in a sea of irrelevance. Orwell feared we would become a captive culture. Huxley feared we would become a trivial culture, preoccupied with some equivalent of the feelies, the orgy porgy, and the centrifugal bumblepuppy . . . In *1984* . . . people are controlled by inflicting pain. In *Brave New World*, they

are controlled by inflicting pleasure. In short, Orwell feared that what we hate will ruin us. Huxley feared that what we love will ruin us.[4]

In our "brave new world" we are bombarded by choices of enjoyments. We feel a large degree of freedom over so much of our lives that we rarely recognize how our thinking has been conditioned to accept things as they are. We accept so much injustice as simply "the way things are," and when we do notice injustice, we feel so overwhelmed and fatigued by the chaos of the overloaded "First World" way of life that we don't know what to do about it. Usually, when someone does muster the mojo to do something about it, they use the systems already in place to address injustice, assuming that they offer the only way to remedy the world's problems. In other words, they vote. Or maybe protest. But they accept the system as it is on its own terms.

But, through the noise, most people still care about the struggle of others. They aren't so selfish that they are content to be fat and happy themselves while others suffer. But as they seek to reach out to help, their actions are often shaped by prevailing myths. Myths are the stories we internalize that help us understand how the world works. Sometimes myths are helpful, but all too often, they serve the principalities and powers.

THE POWER OF MYTHS

My family moved during the summer before I began third grade. I was a shy, chubby lad in a new school. I would often retreat to the school library in those days; it was easier than trying to make friends.

I paged through hundreds of books, but I was most fascinated with mythology and folklore. One book in particular captured my imagination: *D'Aulaire's Book of Norse Myths*. The stories were good, but the illustrations were amazing. When I cracked the cover, I was transported to an enchanted world of ancient tales and epic struggle. The world of the ancient Norse was filled with fantastic creatures and giants and gods. It was much more interesting than this world—a world without myths.

Or is it? Is our modern world free from myths? Perhaps the only ones who cling to myths are religious folks who insist on believing in a Big Sky Daddy?

---

4. Postman, *Amusing Ourselves*, vii–viii.

As I got older, the world became disenchanted. Yet our world is no less filled with myths. Ours are, perhaps, simply more boring. Instead of three elderly Norns determining our fate, it is the Invisible Hand of the market.

It seems misguided (as some of my atheist friends assume) that to be formally "godless" is to escape the realm of myth. Myths, whether consciously linked to spiritual beliefs or not, shape all of our lives—no less today than in the distant past. The myths that seize us today aren't stories of gods and their quests. But with us, just as with the ancients, "myth . . . contains an element of belief, of religious belonging, of the irrational, without which it could never express what it is meant to express for [humanity]."[5] In other words, even though our myths don't outwardly resemble ancient myths, they still function in much the same way. They are the stories and symbols that give shape to our most unchallenged beliefs, that create a sense of collective belonging, that define for us what it most means to be human.

Myths become stories that we no longer question—they provide meaning and direction and shape our imaginations without our choosing them— they are simply "the way things are." In this way, they make the principalities and powers reasonable even when they defy logic. When myths take root in our imaginations, we can no longer imagine our lives without the myths. The most powerful myths are the ones that remain unnamed—they are taken for granted to such an extent that few people ever question them.

Sometimes myths are beautiful stories and ideas that give our world a sense of wonder. Other times, myths are the lies we all agree are truth. Such myths are the often untold stories that legitimize things in this world that are themselves illegitimate.

For good or for ill, myths are the unseen stories by which we navigate our lives. We may be able to name the powers, but how we name them and how we engage them are often determined by our guiding myths. And if the myths of our society are in service to the powers, then we find ourselves in a difficult situation.

EXPOSING FALSE MYTHS

Myths are difficult to expose. They are largely invisible. If, for example, you explain to someone that money doesn't really "exist" (except as a sort of contract printed on a piece of paper) and have value in itself, many folks will struggle to understand what you are saying. So many detrimental

5. Ellul, *New Demons*, 9.

things in our society exist largely because no one realizes that such things need not remain. There are alternatives.

On a hot spring day in 2010, I saw several myths stripped bare. I was participating in a protest outside a government building in South Minneapolis. Hundreds gathered to voice their opposition to a proposed bill that would allow law enforcement to determine an individual's immigration status during any legal "stop." It would, in other words, encourage racial profiling. There was not only a large number of Latin Americans present but allies from other backgrounds as well. It was, for the most part, a typical protest. Government employees furtively peeked out of their office windows while a few police officers guarded the door. The protesters held a variety of signs declaring, "No one is illegal" or "This is what democracy looks like" or "Love knows no borders." Chants were chanted. Fists were raised in rhythm. Songs were sung.

It was what happened next that will forever change my way of understanding immigration. As planned, our group began to march toward Fort Snelling, where a group of Native Americans gathered.

Fort Snelling was built in the 1820s. To many, it is a quaint place to take your family to learn about history. It is a place where middle-aged men can dress up in Civil War uniforms and reenact stuff. It is a cherished monument to the struggle of pioneers and the indomitable American spirit.

But it began as a base from which to subjugate the Dakota Nation. In the 1820s, the primary job of the military in Minnesota was to create space for white settlers. And so they built a fort overlooking the meeting of the Mississippi and Minnesota rivers—a place where the Dakota were created. The United States government built a fort on what one could call the Dakota Garden of Eden. Aggression against the Dakota grew over the decades until the US-Dakota War of 1862. Most Dakota were driven out of the state. On November 13, 1862, about 1,700 of the remaining Dakota people, mostly women and children, were forcibly marched to a concentration camp at Fort Snelling. Several hundred died during the march.

On this hot spring day, Native Americans gathered at Fort Snelling to protest its existence. To them, Fort Snelling wasn't quaint. It was like Auschwitz. Yet most Minnesotans look at Fort Snelling not with feelings of shame but with feelings of pride.

As our group approached Fort Snelling, another group made up of Dakota and Anishinabe and others greeted us. In particular, they greeted those among us who are natives of the Americas.

A Dakota chief, citing tradition and treaty laws, formally welcomed all Latin American people—whether they were "legal" or not—to Minnesota. Furthermore, they were granted unconditional amnesty. The Dakota Nation had made their own immigration reform, declaring "illegal immigrants" legal. They did not grant this hospitality to the others gathered. According to the Dakota, my immigration status was questionable.

In those moments, several very powerful myths were exposed:

- That the land underneath my feet is called "Minnesota" and is a part of a larger piece of land called "the United States." The indigenous peoples of this land had different ways of naming places. The idea that a political entity and the land in which that entity dwells are the same thing is amazingly counterintuitive. Yet we believe it because it is an unquestioned myth.

- That the struggle of Native North Americans exists in the past. Rather, the oppression of the Indigenous peoples of North America continues. The wounds of the past haven't healed; indeed, there are fresh wounds. Most of us remain unaware of the current struggles of Native Americans because we believe the myth that such things remain in the past. Or perhaps we simply don't notice such struggles because the Native population in the US is so small (which is the result of intentional programs of genocide on behalf of state and federal governments).

- That there are a group of people called "illegal immigrants" who need the permission of the United States government to reside in this land. Who has the right to include and exclude? By what right does the United States government set and maintain borders? In his declaration, the Dakota chief exposed the illegitimacy of the US government to declare anyone "illegal"—and, furthermore, suggested that the United States was itself illegal.

No doubt, some of my readers will scoff at this example. One person's unassailable truth is another person's myth, I suppose. Nevertheless, by looking at the world through the eyes of the oppressed (as much as is possible for an educated, white USAmerican man), I saw the world differently. I believe that the teaching and witness of Jesus encourages me to see the world through that lens.

It takes a lifetime of discipleship (for we are all discipled by something) to see the world in such a way that our current political realities mediate our way of seeing the world. We rarely, if ever, question the myth that there is a land—including all of its soil and rocks and lakes and wildlife—that *is* the United States. That story shapes our imaginations so powerfully that it is hard to see the land as itself. And there are other powerful myths that similarly mediate our relationship with the land, with the people who dwell in the land, and with the God who created the land.

This is how imperial myths usually work. They cast their spell on our imaginations in such a way that injustices become part of "the way things are." And they leave us justified in our participation in "the way things are." Even when we come to the realization that they should be otherwise, we are left feeling impotent and unable to see a way forward.

When someone challenges the dominant myths of a society, the Empire strikes back. This happened to the prophets. It happened to Jesus. It will happen to you, should you start poking at the myths that hold our society together. Poke anyway; God loves us too much for us to be enslaved by false myths.

TOWARD REPENTANCE

It isn't easy to follow Jesus with the weight of two thousand years of imperialism in the name of Jesus bearing upon one's soul. What are our options?

The first option is to renounce your faith. Tell yourself that it is a problem for religious people and simply decide to become irreligious. Or that it is a problem for Christians, and decide you are no longer a Christian. By a simple shift in beliefs, you can have clean hands . . .

But what will that accomplish? By denouncing Christ do you somehow get yourself off the hook of Empire? Does becoming an agnostic automatically disentangle one from complicity? It is one thing to become an agnostic or atheist out of conviction. It is quite another to do so in an attempt to remove responsibility.

You could, I suppose, follow up such a renunciation with a bold act of becoming an insurrectionist or a deep activist. That, to me, is an honest way of coming to terms with Empire. It makes sense that if you choose to undo the damage of Christendom by denouncing Christ, then you must also aggressively commit yourself to bringing healing to the legacy you've inherited. It has shaped you; it is part of you. You weren't born with a blank slate in a world of your own choosing. You were born into this place and this time with particular privileges and histories.

The second option is willing apathy. You can let yourself grow numb and apathetic about such troubling things as modern Empire, past atrocities, and the steady march toward social and environmental degradation. You can set Christianity aside as a clean ideal that helps you cope. You can embrace the imperial Christianity you've inherited. Simply tell yourself that "it isn't so bad" and that "there's nothing I can do anyway" and relax. I'm assuming that many Christians will take this option.

The third option is the most popular: Simply believe that it is enough to be "aware." Tell yourself that it is enough to be aware of the problems of the world, the challenges they present to your faith, and take comfort in knowing that you are one of the few Christians who really "get it."

The fourth option is, perhaps, the least popular and most messy: You can repent of this thing we call Christianity and seek to follow Jesus. I am convinced that this is the best way forward. Jesus' way was an anti-imperial way. That is why it is so powerful as a co-opted force *for* Empire.

I want to clarify something here. I am in no way advocating something as simplistic as becoming "spiritual but not religious." There is a tendency for many folks to reject the church while still affirming Jesus. There is a danger in that of simply becoming a Denomination of One, with a personal deity of your own imagination that cannot be challenged by anyone else. I'm advocating a much deeper sort of repentance—one that requires deep honesty.

Our imaginations too easily fall into old patterns. We see repentance as the action of individuals. I'm not advocating that we walk away from the church and "go it alone." Rather, I believe the church needs to repent of Christianity. We must confess our sins together—to name our complicity with systems of oppression. And we need to move forward into wholeness and healing together.

CHAPTER TWO GROUP GUIDE

 Summary

Our society pushes us to have an abstracted view of reality. Instead of seeing a world of people and creation, we get distracted by systems and ideas that we confuse with reality. These systems are called "the powers" by the Apostle Paul. And these ideas become myths—stories we so assume to be true that they mediate our experience of reality. It is these powers and myths that cause us to live in an oppressive system without questioning it too much.

Discussion Questions

1. The author asserts, "We are bombarded by choices of enjoyments. We feel a large degree of freedom over so much of our lives that we rarely recognize how our thinking has been conditioned to accept things as they are." Does this ring true for you?

2. In this chapter, the author recounts an experience at Fort Snelling where several myths were exposed. What other myths continue to captivate our imaginations?

3. Which of the four responses listed in the section "Toward Repentance" draws you the most?

Group Practice

Set aside at least fifteen minutes. Ask everyone to think of a big story our society tells that they once believed to be true but have since rejected, particularly something that has been significant in their lives. Ask them to journal about it (provide paper, if necessary). Then go around and allow everyone to share with the group.

Close with a time of silence or prayer.

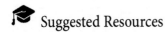 Suggested Resources

The New Demons, by Jacques Ellul
An Ethic for Christians and Other Aliens in a Strange Land, by William Stringfellow
The Powers Trilogy, by Walter Wink

SWEET JESUS

I long for you to appear
Sweet Jesus
To whisper sweet nothings into my ear
Sweet Jesus
And to forgive my sins, my dear
Sweet Jesus
Like drinking too much beer
Being insincere
And forgetting you all year
Sweet Jesus

Show me the narrow path
Sweet Jesus
Away from your father's wrath
Sweet Jesus
Give my soul a bath
Sweet Jesus
So that I can laugh
For all the junk I hath
From plying $atan's math
Sweet Jesus

You make me white as snow
Sweet Jesus
So merrily I go
Sweet Jesus
To maintain the status quo
Sweet Jesus
Like keeping down the low
Having too much dough
And killing all my foes
Sweet Jesus

3

Repenting of Christianity

God, rid me of God.

—Meister Eckhart

My faith collapsed with my mother's lungs.

I spent my late teens caring for my dying mother. After years of struggling with emphysema, my mom's lungs failed. Thankfully, with the help of medication and an oxygen tank, she was able to survive for the few years it took to get a lung transplant. Her surgery was successful, but the anti-rejection meds made her puffy, and she always seemed dangerously close to death. But she was alive . . . until she started smoking again. Within a few months of lighting up for the first time in years, she was dead. She died when I was nineteen.

While other teenagers were out getting drunk in ice houses (which is totally a thing in Minnesota) or playing CB tag (Google it), I took care of my mother. The depressingness of those years seemed to fit the spirit of the early nineties. My life read like an overwrought script about a young man's struggle with depression-laden absurdity. I was Gilbert Grape. I smelled like Teen Spirit. Gone was the optimism of the eighties, only to be replaced with the cynical honesty of the early nineties.

I didn't go to college after high school, even though my ACT scores were the best of my graduating class. Family first. I didn't have many friends—many moved away after graduation. I was afraid to leave my mother alone. I was terrified that she would die while I was gone. On those rare occasions when I'd go out with friends, my mother would shame me for staying away too long. "It is a good thing I didn't die while you were out with your friends," she would say.

My mother did let me have a part-time job, however. I needed money for a car and clothes, and the money she got only covered the basics: rent and food. I had what is perhaps the most soul-numbing job imaginable. I worked about fifteen hours a week sweeping a warehouse. It was a 40,000-square-foot freezer that housed only one thing: McDonald's french fries.

I was supposed to take a break every hour, because of the cold. I recall one time my supervisor asked me, "Why don't you ever take breaks? It is freezing in there, you're supposed to take a break sometimes."

I responded, "What's the point?"

And then I would get into my car and drive home. My car was as sad as my job. It was an old Datsun 200SX with failing breaks. It was pale blue and rusty. The driver's side seat was propped forward by a broken hard-shelled suitcase. There was no muffler. But the stereo worked.

Since my job gave me a lot of time alone to think, my mind would often ruminate over my miserable lot in life. I felt abandoned. I was the youngest of six children, yet I was left to care for my dying mother. I was a bright kid, yet I stayed in my small town while friends left for college or careers. My church, which had once given my life meaning, was going through a split. I felt abandoned by family, friends, and church.

I felt abandoned by God. The earlier years of my faith had been marked by deep feelings of conviction. God had seemed close to me—sometimes overwhelmingly so. But during this season, I felt nothing. Only drab loneliness.

One day, I drove home to my dying mother in my death-car after sweeping a freezer that held little slivers of frozen potato which would later get a hot oil bath and be eaten by fat faces. It was a cloudy day. This was my life.

My mother and I lived in a subsidized apartment near the trailer park on the north side of town. The walls were white, the carpet beige. I did my best to keep the apartment clean, but my mother was a hoarder. Soda cans (she drank Squirt) were strewn around the couch, my mother's nest. She had a bedroom, but she only used it for storage. She preferred the convenience of the couch—with its proximity to the television and the refrigerator—to the privacy of a bedroom.

Normally when I got home, I would go to the fridge, grab a soda, and proceed to sit down in my chair to watch television with my mother. It was the closest thing to bonding I had with her; we watched *Days of Our Lives* together.

But on this day, I only mumbled to her as I walked directly to my room. Earlier, as I swept dust off a cold concrete floor, I had reflected upon my sad life and decided that I would formally renounce Christ.

I wanted to do it properly. I cleared space in the middle of my bedroom floor. I stripped naked and lay down upon the beige carpet of my bedroom, eyes staring up at the ceiling. After a time of silence, I began speaking words of rejection to God, committing intentional acts of blasphemy. If God had forsaken me, I would forsake God.

I'll spare you the details of my attempted apostasy. I blasphemed, forsook, and un-prayed for about an hour. When it was over, I was tired and numb; there was no release. No closure. I was just a naked, depressed teenager lying on the floor.

But then, in the silence, something happened. I felt the presence of Christ. It wasn't accompanied by joy; it was accompanied by deeper feelings of sadness. In my soul, I knew that this deepening sadness was not my own, but the sorrow of Christ. Christ had come to commiserate. In those moments I knew he felt as I felt. He seemed as fed up, as angry, as depressed. He was with me in the midst of my grey season.

As I lay in silent sadness, Jesus said, "Let it all go. Forsake it all. But you can't forsake me, because I haven't abandoned you. You can reject everything—the church, your theology, everything, but I'm still here." And then things drifted back to normal. I was left on the floor in silent sadness.

My life continued in the same sad way, but something small had shifted. I look back upon that day as the reason I'm a Christian. By forsaking Christ, I found Christ. Or, to be more precise, he found me.

EVERYTHING THAT IS NOT GOD

In recent years, I've begun reading the works of French activist, mystic, and philosopher Simone Weil. She's one of those intellectuals that is often quoted but rarely read. She defies easy categorization. A third of the time, I am struck with her brilliance. During the other two-thirds, I alternate between feelings of active boredom and mental irritation. I'd like to share with you one of her brilliant (yet irritating) statements. I share it because it speaks to my experience of failed apostasy:

> It is not for man [*sic*] to seek, or even to believe in God. He has only to refuse to believe in everything that is not God. This refusal does not presuppose belief. It is enough to recognize, what is obvious to any mind, that all the goods of this world, past, present, or future, real or imaginary, are finite and limited and radically incapable of satisfying the desire which burns perpetually within us for an infinite and perfect good . . . It is not a matter of self-questioning or searching. A man has only to persist in his refusal, and one day or another God will come to him.[1]

That day—when I yelled at the ceiling in defiance—was the first time it had ever occurred to me that the Christ of my imagination might bear little or no resemblance to the living Christ. It was—and still is—an unsettling notion. But I have become comfortable with being unsettled. That is, I believe, the nature of faith.

Our notions of God are often the biggest obstacles to knowing God. For much of my life, my Christianity has been a string of idolatrous ideas that have separated me from Christ—ideas that keep the untamed God safely distant.

I have come to know Christ in the letting go of Christ. My prayer has become the same as thirteenth-century mystic Meister Eckhart's: "God, rid me of God."

God is found in the letting go of God. We cannot cling to God. Rather, we find that God clings to us. In this clinging, we continue to insist that God exist in a particular way and do particular things. That makes God our slave, and as a result, we remain enslaved to our God-thoughts.

So much of my Christianity (and I believe the historic expression of Christianity over the past two thousand years) has been an attempt to keep Christ in a cage. We don't want a free, living Christ, one we cannot control.

We treat the living Jesus like a doddering fool, humored to his face yet secretly disdained. The dead Jesus, who has never lived, is our god. This dead Jesus is a compilation and distillation of our self-serving ideals. We gladly worship this Jesus, since he is a personification of our most apparent desires and dreams—desires and dreams that have been shaped by our shared myths.

If we want to follow Christ, we need to repent of our Christianity.

1. Weil, *On Science*, 126.

Granted, there is no such "thing" as Christianity—Christianity has always been a messy constellation of ideas and traditions. Even the apostles Peter and Paul disagreed over what it was all about.[2] And things have only gotten more complicated. Today, it is impossible to speak of a single thing called "Christianity," since it is a fluid and flexible social grouping of more than a billion people who rarely, if ever, fit into any textbook definitions. While this thing we try to call "Christianity" is really a huge messy pile of constantly changing ideas and traditions, few (if any) of those ideas and traditions remain untainted by the stain of domination.

So, when I say "Christianity" I am referring generally to the dominant strands of Christianity that make up the bulk of the Western tradition. In particular, my experience is primarily with Protestant Christianity in America. I grew up in Minnesota among Lutherans, came to faith among charismatics and Pentecostals, came of age among nondenominational evangelicals, went to seminary with Baptists, began to ask questions with emergents, and became a pastor among Mennonites. And while I don't claim to be an expert on any of these traditions, I believe that the challenges and encouragements of this book apply to each—and more.

For two millennia, we Christians have been complicit in the deepest sins of Western civilization. No doubt, Christianity has contributed to our triumphs as well. As I read history, I find countless stories that inspire me to become a more loving human being. But few would disagree that the historical reality of Christianity falls far short of our ideals. Given the wide margin by which we have, collectively, fallen short, one must question whether or not our stated ideals are the ones we actually hold.

This gap is problematic. Christianity is a religion that places embodiment at the center. Ours isn't a religion of disembodied ideals but of flesh-and-blood realities. Whatever we are in practice is what we value most in our hearts. If, as Paul suggests in 2 Corinthians 3, our lives are to be like living epistles from Christ, what happens when we more closely resemble a horror story? Or, at best, a dark comedy? Who, then, is our author?

Why is it that when critics point out the ugly story of Christian domination, so many Christians argue that those examples aren't "real" Christianity? And when self-described Christians commit genocide, oppress the poor, subjugate women, or simply act wickedly, they aren't *real* Christians; their actions have nothing to do with their alleged faith.

2. For example, in Galatians 2, Paul recounts an argument with Peter over whether or not Gentiles should follow Jewish customs.

And so, successive generations of Christians can avoid responsibility. We can distance ourselves from the sins of the past without having to examine whether or not the same genocidal/racist/sexist/classist tendencies are embedded within the fabric of our own Christianity.

I'm fairly certain that Jesus' vision wasn't to leave us a bunch of nifty ideals in a book. His vision wasn't a set of disembodied doctrines—it is something we live out. And if the majority of the ways it has been lived out have been enmeshed with a history of domination or oppression, then that is the Christian witness to the world. Yes, we can all point to some glorious idea in a book and say that is the real Christianity, but what good does that do anybody?

So, while there may be a disembodied, completely pure definition of Christianity that exists as some sort of platonic ideal, the closest thing to such Christianity is rarely, if ever, seen in the real world. Our task should be less about defining an ever purer utopian Christianity and more about embodying a tangible way of love.

And so, we find ourselves with a dilemma. Most of us can point to a loving ideal—a disembodied utopia of Christianity—but, for most people throughout history, Christianity has been complicit in bringing injustice. The most public and prolific examples of Christianity in our world today are in opposition to our ideals.

Jesus has become a tool of Empire. Those who conquer often adopt the mythologies of the conquered; it allows them to maintain the status quo even as they open controlled spaces for folks to speak of revolution. Whether we like it or not, even radical Christian stories have been appropriated into the mythologies of Western civilization. We live in a society where the largest military machine in the history of the world can erect a monument to Dr. King. We live in a world where a president can name Jesus Christ as his favorite philosopher and, shortly thereafter, launch two wars.

Our ways of understanding liberation, freedom, goodness, prosperity, and happiness have largely been shaped by the American Dream (or its other national variations). The ways that Christianity has been corrupted as a tool to captivate our imaginations in service of Western civilization run deep.

THREE WAYS OF OPTING OUT

Repenting of our Christianity, however, isn't as easy as simply "opting out." Over the past several years, I've met a number of people who, when they realize the dark history of Christendom, simply walk away from Christianity, sometimes in the belief that their de-conversion gets them off the hook for sins perpetrated in the name of Jesus Christ. While I respect that some honestly migrate away from Christianity, I don't believe it is intellectually honest to opt out as a way of removing shame; one doesn't need to be a professing Christian to have had their imagination shaped by Christendom. Even though I didn't embrace Christianity until my teens, I have been shaped by Christian ideas and stories (though it would be more precise to call them quasi-Christian USAmerican imperialist narratives) my whole life. Christendom, rather than Christ, has shaped how I think and act and feel.

There is another way folks try to opt out; by laying claim to a more radical Christianity, many foolishly assume that they've changed sides. They jump from team "Empire" to team "Radical." This is very much akin to a white dude somehow claiming he is, in fact, no longer a racist after taking a college course addressing racism (or participating in a racial reconciliation workshop). I've identified myself as a "radical" Christian for about ten years. At no point has my racism or sexism or classism magically disappeared. It doesn't work that way. Racism, sexism, and classism are ways of seeing the world; they aren't simply positions one holds. So even if you suddenly change your mind, it takes a lifetime to change your lens.

In their effort to change sides, some attempt to opt out of their complicity in Christian imperialism by joining a more radical form of Christianity. This was part of my own rationale for joining the Mennonites. But Mennonites, despite a relationship to Empire that is relatively unique among Christians, are still shaped adversely by Christendom. For example, while most Mennonites reject violence, few Mennonites challenge economic exploitation. And even that commitment to nonviolence is eroding over time. Furthermore, to speak personally, joining a pacifist tradition didn't magically eradicate the violence in my own heart. Escaping to a more radical Christianity in and of itself is not a solution to our complicity with an imperial form of Christianity.

A third way of opting out is more subtle. If the three responses to a threat are flight, fight, or freeze (the previous two options being flight and fight), then the freeze response is to simply be crushed by a mountain of shame. I want to spend a bit more time discussing this response because I believe it is the most pervasive way of opting out.

Shame is anger turned inward. It can even become self-hatred. And, usually, that self-anger comes from a mixture of lies and truth. We have all internalized lies that cause us to hate ourselves. But shame can also stem from being confronted with a hard truth.

For example, many men I know feel a particular sense of shame around sex. I'm the same way. Deep inside, part of me believes that sex is dirty. It is wrong. I believe this because so much in our society reinforces this view—from the way media depicts sex as "transgressive" or "naughty" to the way television portrays men as pigs who "only think of one thing." Moreover, many of the messages we hear from our churches about sex (when sex is actually talked about) further enhance both our confusion and the association between sex and shame. For example, I was taught as a teenager never to hug a woman front-to-front but to give them a "side hug." Because of such conditioning, I have to struggle as a married man with a tendency to view sexual longings and urges as shameful and wrong.

When one holds such a secret shame—one that is based upon lies—it is hard to hear the truth. The truth about the complexities of sexuality and the goodness of sexual desire is hard for me to really embrace. It is also hard for me to hear the truth about the high percentage of men who can be sexually abusive or unfaithful. Speaking truth to the lies doesn't necessarily lead to liberation. At first it just heightened my experience of shame.

Another example can be seen at a national level. We all know, at least superficially, of the dark history of the United States. Most of us, to some degree, feel shame about that. Indeed, I have some internalized anger over the privileges I get in this society simply by virtue of being a heterosexual white man.

It is true: the villains who enslaved and subjugated are long dead. Yet, they are convenient scapegoats. When I look at this nation, I see some of the fruits of that oppression and I have more access to enjoy those fruits. I feel ashamed. The shame comes from the truth that I am complicit in continuing the legacy of oppression, even if that complicity isn't active. But the lie that contributes to that shame is that "this is just the way it is" or that "justice is impossible" or even "white men don't have a role to play in seeking justice."

Repentance isn't dwelling on shame. It is working through the shame. By confessing the truth while rejecting lies we can begin to see a way forward. By confessing the goodness of sex while rejecting the lies that sex is dirty, I can learn how to worship God and love my wife with a liberated sexuality. By confessing the dark history of my society and the painful truth of my present privilege while, at the same time, continuing to learn my role in seeking justice, I can find true joy, rather than a false joy based upon avoidance of the truth. When we work through shame, it becomes revolutionary.

Our society has become expert at avoiding shame, rather than working through shame. When we can name that shame, recognize our internalized anger, and direct the anger at its most appropriate target, we can create space for liberation. Anger at ourselves for inaction can spur us toward action in the future. Anger at a system that marginalizes people and steals their voices can move us to tear that system down.

When avoidance of shame becomes pathology, we demonize truth tellers. This is why Israel killed its prophets. It is why we kill ours (or imprison or ostracize them). Let us listen to the voices coming to us from the wilderness, calling us to repentance.

Feeling shame is an invitation to repentance. It is the recognition that something is wrong that manifests as self-anger. If we can open up space to examine that shame, to talk about that shame, and to confess that shame, then we will be on the path of repentance. And when we collectively repent as our response to collective shame, we are on the path to revolution.

The roots of Empire go deep. Learning a new script takes a lifetime. If I am going to be faithful to the way of Jesus (which is tricky, since my understanding of Jesus and his way has been so shaped by oppressive systems), I need to confess the brokenness of my Christianity in full recognition of how much it has shaped my identity. It is, for better or worse, part of who I am.

So, I don't think it is honest to "opt out" by simply rejecting Christianity (that would be like washing the outside of a cup but leaving the inside dirty) or joining some radical Christian enclave (as if such a thing actually existed) or simply going numb as a response to crushing shame (which serves no positive purpose whatsoever). Instead, we need to repent of Christianity.

Repentance is not an event or an emotion; it is an ongoing invitation to engage the world differently—to see the world the way God does and act accordingly. Repenting of Christianity means adopting a posture of honest confession as we seek a better way.

A story is told about a respected scholar who leaves his university to pursue enlightenment. Eventually, he visits the home of a renowned Zen master.

"Please, master, I have come to find enlightenment," he says as the master answers his door. The master welcomes him and, good host that he is, offers the scholar some tea.

They sit. The master begins pouring tea into the scholar's cup. The cup fills, and yet he keeps pouring—until it overflows. He keeps pouring as tea spills onto the table and onto the floor.

At this, the scholar exclaims, "The cup is overflowing! You can't pour any more into it!"

The Master replies, "Like this cup, you are overflowing with your own ideas. How can I show you enlightenment if you are already full?"

We think we are open to learning the way of Jesus, but our cup is already full of our own ideas. Unfortunately, we don't notice that it is full. As a result, many of us can spend our lives pouring sermons and Scripture readings into our minds, but they simply spill back out. At best, we merely baptize our own thoughts and suggest that they are Jesus'. Our lives are full to the brim with societal myths. The stories read to us as children, the toys we played with, the television we've watched, the books we've read, the advertisements we've absorbed, the laws we've followed—all of these have shaped us. And now our minds can't even imagine the alternatives.

We need to empty our cups. We need to repent of the myths that crowd our imaginations. We need to repent of our Christianity.

Gelassenheit is a German word from the medieval mystics. For some, it was a sort of inner quiet that led to detachment from worldly concerns. But for others, particularly the Anabaptists, *Gelassenheit* was practical. *Gelassenheit* isn't simply about an individual's inner spiritual life but their relationships with others.

Gelassenheit is about ridding one's life of all obstacles to love of God and neighbor. As the early Anabaptist Hans Haffner wrote in his devotional tract *Concerning a True Soldier of Christ*, "When we truly realize the love of God we will be ready to give up ["give up" is an English translation of *Gelassenheit*] for love's sake even what God has given us."[3] Love is the one thing that remains because, while love often feels like an abstraction, it is the most real. John taught that "God is love."[4] Paul taught that everything will pass away, yet faith, hope, and love will remain (and the greatest of these is love).[5] Jesus said that the Law and the Prophets all hang on our love of God and neighbor.[6]

3. Haffner, *Concerning a True Soldier of Christ*.

4. 1 John 4:8.

5. 1 Cor 13.

6. Matt 22:34–40.

When I say we need to repent of Christianity, I am advocating that we let go of beliefs and structures and institutions and buildings and money and stories—everything that we put upon Jesus—and ask, "Is this the way of love?" or "Is this separating me from God and my neighbor?"

What we need now, more than ever, is a new spirituality of *Gelassenheit*: one that seeks to remove all of the obstacles to our love. One that understands the intrinsic relationship between love of God and love of others. A spirituality that will gladly set aside all things—even if they are gifts from God—for love's sake.

This isn't to say that we should embrace a simplistic, naive spirituality devoid of stories and structures. I'm simply advocating that we recognize them as abstractions that must be yielded to God. Otherwise, they will become the idols we worship in place of God.

I need to repent of Christianity in order to love God and neighbor. But I cannot repent of it by simply walking away—it is a part of me. And so, I cannot repent of Christianity without naming myself as a Christian.

I am a Christian, I repent of Christianity. This is my religion. I will keep saying that for the rest of my life. The moment I stop yielding my Christianity to God is the moment I stop loving.

If we attempt to bring about social justice without a life of repentance, we will presumptuously carry our imperialism with us into the margins. When Empire enters the margins, it is usually considered "colonization." If we are going to be agents of God's love, we have to yield our hearts to God for decolonization. This is, painfully, a lifelong process. I don't assume that I'll ever be free from subtly colonizing habits and attitudes. And I certainly won't ever entirely escape from the social privileges afforded to me by virtue of my status as an educate white USAmerican male. Nevertheless, out of love for God and neighbor, everything—even my Christianity—needs to yield.

Gelassenheit is a spirituality for those of us who follow Jesus in the Empire. Apart from such a spirituality, we are left with either dogmatism, on the one hand, or Marxist materialism (the idea that we simply need to attend to human structures in our quest for justice) on the other. The former clings so much that it remains willfully unable to embrace liberation. The latter assumes that it has moved past Christianity (when in reality, often such folks are merely evangelical Marxists).

But in all things, may we give up for love's sake even what God has given us.

My favorite novel, *Silence*, follows a Portuguese priest, Rodrigues, on a dangerous mission to Japan (during the Tokugawa shogunate). Rodrigues is sent to investigate the growing number of faithful apostatizing, particularly Father Ferreira, a famous missionary. After a time in Japan, Rodrigues is (through the deceit of a friend) turned in to authorities.

Rodrigues holds to a triumphant European Christ. In his faithfulness, he clings to Jesus even amidst torture. He continues in his steadfastness as apostate Christians are tortured in front of him. He remains pure even as everyone else forsakes Christ.

But the stakes are raised; he is told that if he doesn't forsake Christ by stepping on a fumie (which is an image of the crucified Christ) many of the apostate Christians will be killed. Does he cling faithfully to the Christ of the fumie, or does he forsake him, thus saving the others? In this act he is confronted with an entirely different understanding of Christ, whose voice speaks after a long silence:

> The first rays of the dawn appear. The light shines on his long neck stretched out like a chicken and upon the bony shoulders. The priest grasps the fumie with both hands bringing it close to his eyes. He would like to press to his own face that face trampled on by so many feet. With saddened glance he stares intently at the man in the center of the fumie, worn down and hollow with the constant trampling. A tear is about to fall from his eye. "Ah," he says trembling, "the pain!"
>
> The priest raises his foot. In it he feels a dull, heavy pain. This is no mere formality. He will now trample on what he has considered the most beautiful thing in his life, on what he has believed most pure, on what is filled with the ideals and dreams of man. How his foot aches! And then the Christ in bronze speaks to the priest: "Trample! Trample! I more than anyone know of the pain in your foot. Trample! It was to be trampled on by men that I was born into this world. It was to share men's pain that I carried my cross."
>
> The priest placed his foot on the fumie. Dawn broke. And far in the distance the cock crew.[7]

Are we willing to forsake our image of Christ in order to become as Christ? Are we willing to repent of our Christianity in order to be the love of Christ in our world?

---

7. Endo, *Silence*, 171.

CHAPTER THREE GROUP GUIDE

 Summary

To be faithful to Jesus, we need to forsake the image of Jesus we cling to in our imagination. The greatest enemy to the Way of Jesus has often been the religion created to honor Jesus. We must let go of everything that has become an idol and reengage the offensive and liberating Jesus in the Gospels.

Discussion Questions

1. Which of the "three ways of opting out" do you most recognize within yourself?

2. The author writes, "When avoidance of shame becomes pathology, we demonize truth tellers. This is why Israel killed its prophets. It is why we kill ours (or imprison or ostracize them)." Can you think of any demonized truth tellers? What uncomfortable truth are they sharing?

3. What are the promises and perils of taking seriously the author's invitation to "repent of Christianity"?

Group Practice: Honoring the Truth Tellers

This is a time to honor the truth tellers. While everyone else sits silently with their eyes closed, have someone read (slowly and thoughtfully) Luke 6:12–26. After a few minutes of silence, invite everyone to begin to speak into the silence, saying the name of a truth teller (either someone they know from history or someone from their own personal lives).

Close with a time of silence or prayer.

Suggested Resources

Silence, by Shusaku Endo (also available as a recently released film by Martin Scorsese)

My Mind's Ambition

I place my mind on the dewy grass
where it lies, naked pink and shivering
like a newborn sparrow
crying for comfort.

But no comfort comes,
only chilly death.
And then, to be devoured
by a wild dog.

In time, after my mind breaks down
it will flow into dog blood and fuel howls.
Still later, as dog shit
my mind will feed dandelions.

Oh, to be dandelion fluff
carried on a summer night's breeze
is my mind's ambition.

4

Embracing the Mysticism of Children

Truly I tell you, unless you change and become like little children,
you will never enter the kingdom of heaven.

—MATTHEW 18:3

ONE LATE DECEMBER AFTERNOON, I stood with my wife and my son Jonas—then three and a half years old—in line at a cheap all-you-can-eat Asian buffet restaurant. Like most buffet restaurants, the food was both enticing and disgusting at the same time. This particular restaurant boasts the largest seating capacity in Minneapolis. The convergence of cheap food, wide selection, and ample seating makes it a convenient choice for parents looking for a no-hassle approach to feeding their kids. I'm not alone in this opinion; about a third of the diners during this particular visit were kids. Predictably, most of these kids seemed fatter than average.

As I stood in line, I felt the sort of guilt that is unique to parents. It is that feeling that comes when one realizes, "If I keep doing this, I'm going to ruin my kid." Nevertheless, on this occasion (as often happens with parents), my desire for convenience trumped my dull pangs of guilt. And so we stayed in line, slowly inching forward, waiting to be seated as my wife, Amy, went off to the bathroom.

Near the entrance was an entirely too large water fountain: clearly an attempt to "class things up." Jonas wanted to throw a penny in.

When Amy got back from the bathroom, she held our place in line while Jonas and I went to the cheesy plastic-rock fountain. I had two pennies in my pocket. Jonas jumped up and down with excitement as I placed them in his eager hand. Still caught up in the excitement, he threw them both in at the same time. My son has never been the sort of kid to draw out enjoyable experiences.

"What did you wish for?" I asked.

Jonas scrunched up his face a little. That's his "thinking face."

I added, "It's okay if you forgot. The wish still counts if you can come up with one before wish-time runs out." I was, of course, bending the truth about wish protocol.

Almost immediately, his face *unscrunched*. He looked into my eyes. "That Jesus could be alive," he said.

His answer surprised me. I had told him the usual Bible stories: that Jesus was born in a manger, that he healed people and told us to love each other, and that he died. But I had always stressed that Jesus rose from the dead—he was alive now and someday he would come for everyone who had died (like grandma Gloria and great-grandma Mildred) and give them new life.

I began to worry that someone was trying to undo my attempts to shape my son's theology. I started rounding up suspects in my mind.

"But Jonas, Jesus *is* alive!" I said with joyful certainty. I thought he would nod, the way children sometimes do when you remind them of things they have forgotten. But his response shook me. I remember it often.

"Jesus is dead in the buildings and in the cities and in the outside. But he is alive in our hearts."

And then he skipped away to stand next to his mommy in line.

I have no idea what my son was thinking. Little kids say silly things; sometimes those silly things sound wise. Perhaps there is wisdom in silliness. Nevertheless, his statement went straight to my heart. In that moment, I was struck with the conviction that if Jesus doesn't dwell in my own heart, I will not see him anywhere else. If I claim that Jesus lives, then he must live in me.

Upon hearing this story, a friend directed me to a quote from medieval German mystic Meister Eckhart. It affirmed and echoed the words of my son: "We are celebrating the feast of the Eternal Birth which God the Father has borne and *never ceases to bear* in all eternity . . . But if it takes not place in me, what avails it? Everything lies in this, that it should take place in me."[1]

We can condemn the brokenness of the world around us. We can long for a new world—one full and complete and happy. But if the seed of that new world is not in us—if it is not in me—what hope do we have? Jesus is dead if he is not alive in our hearts.

Perhaps my son Jonas is a little mystic. Or perhaps he, like all children, makes strange, unexpected connections between words and ideas.

Little kids tend to use words like they use blocks—in ways that seem abstract, disorganized. They show you something that looks like modern art—angular, with discordant colors—and happily proclaim, "Look, Daddy, a pirate ship!"

Such emerging imaginations are often stifled and constrained by social convention. By the time they enter elementary school, children have learned that pirate ships are brown, that they float in blue water, and that they are, well, boat-shaped. To an extent, this conformity of imagination is good. Children need to learn how to navigate the world in ways that keep them safe, respectful of other people, and patient in the face of challenges. The job of parents and guardians is helping them focus on those things that are good, while helping them say no to those things that are bad or harmful.

But there is a downside to this conformity. Not all of our social conventions are wise or true. As we grow, our pirate-ship aesthetics aren't the only things that get shaped by our society. What once was an imaginative possibility becomes an impossibility. This is okay when the imaginative possibility is being able to reach the moon by climbing a tree. But it is disastrous when we disregard other childish notions: like the belief that everyone should be able to live in a home, or that coins are just shiny toys, or that boundaries on maps are just pretend (all things my son Jonas believes). This isn't instinct; we have to be conditioned to think that not everyone can have a place to live or that money has value or that there is a place called the United States that is governed by a small percentage of predominantly white men in a place far away. Let's be honest: which perspective is truer?

The mind of the child is largely unconstrained. They have eyes to see the world in ways that their parents no longer can. Children aren't stifled by shame or guilt or propriety or politeness. They have to learn those things

---

1. Quoted in Underhill, *Mysticism*, 122.

(usually from their parents). They are feral. And we domesticate them.[2] Often this domestication enslaves their minds and hearts to ideas that render them unable to experience the fullness of the world.

In many important ways, children see the world around them in a far truer light than their parents. They see the world with an unfettered imagination. Within our spiritual tradition, such unfettering is the province of the prophets and the mystics.

The prophets have an imagination for what the world *could* be. They remind us that things don't have to be as they are. The mystics see the world differently; they see a reality that others miss. The prophet exposes lies while the mystic reveals the truth. Both are required for liberation.

Traditionally, mysticism is defined as having an unmediated encounter with the Divine. Mystics live in a world where the veil between heaven and earth is extremely thin. All layers between the mystic and God are stripped away and the mystic experiences God's presence.

The stripping away of layers—the collapsing of spiritual distance—can happen in all kinds of ways. Some mystics encounter God alone in their room. But others experience the presence of God in the face of a stranger. Still others encounter God in nature. In all of these experiences, mysticism isn't otherworldly. It is about encountering the living God wherever God may be. Mysticism collapses the distance between a person and God, between people, and between a person and the rest of creation. At its best, mysticism points toward a life free from abstraction, where you simply see what is.

Because of this, many mystical movements have been on the forefront of social justice. Mystics often see beyond the myths of their society and, in refusing the power of those myths, are able to embody lives of justice. The French mystic and philosopher Simone Weil once wrote, "Truth is too dangerous to touch, it is an explosive." Perhaps this is why mystics have often been ostracized, existing in the margins either by force or by choice. Their experiences threaten to invalidate or destroy the structures and layers that the establishment clings to for its survival. So, when I use the word *mystic*, I

---

2. In his introduction to Paulo Freire's classic text *Pedagogy of the Oppressed*, theologian Richard Shaull writes, "Education either functions as an instrument which is used to facilitate integration of the younger generation into the logic of the present system and bring about conformity to it, *or* it becomes 'the practice of freedom,' the means by which men and women deal critically and creatively with reality and discover how to participate in the transformation of their world" (*Pedagogy of the Oppressed*, 72).

mean those people who see the world with spiritual eyes and, therefore, see things for what they truly are.

There is a danger in walking the path of the prophet apart from that of the mystic. If we attempt to transform the world around us without a renewed imagination, we are likely to repeat the cycle of injustice in fresh ways. Likewise, there is a danger in walking the path of the mystic apart from that of the prophet: that we will move inward without attending to the injustices around us.

Through the eyes of my son, I see the world differently. But I also recognize that the world as it is need not be his inheritance.

Children live in worlds as large as their imagination. And, unfortunately, so do adults. Our problem is not simply that our world is a broken place. Our problem is also that we live in too small a world, where our imaginations cannot see a way forward. We accept what is all too readily.

When Jesus says, "Truly I tell you, whoever does not receive the kingdom of God as a little child will never enter it," he is likely talking about the need for disciples to embrace the vulnerable posture of children, to be in solidarity with the weakest in society. But I often wonder if, perhaps, Jesus also understood that the naive, innocent minds of children are uniquely able to believe in divine impossibilities like the Kingdom of God.

If we are going to enter the Kingdom of God, we need to have childlike imaginations. Our way of seeing the world perpetuates what we see in the world. If we accept the dehumanizing, dominating, destructive patterns of our world as "the way things are," then we cannot help reinforcing those patterns.

If children are mystics, then mysticism is not the domain of a detached, esoteric elite. Rather, mysticism is for all of us. The unexpected collapsing of the distances between God, human beings, and the rest of creation is something all can experience. For many, mystical experiences are rare. As Dorothy Sölle suggests, "By banishing [mystical experiences] from our children, we destroy them within ourselves at the same moment."[3] We live in a world devoid of mystical possibilities because we do not nurture them in our children. Nor do we recognize them in our communities. We have built a prison free from wonder.

Yet there is hope. Sölle writes, "When we start digging up the buried mysticism of childhood, the feeling of oneness and of being overcome

3. Sölle, *Silent Cry*, 13.

arises anew. Memory clings to little, insignificant details."[4] In my own experiences, my ability to see the world through God's eyes begins with remembering childhood moments when wonder was a regular part of my life. By remembering my childhood, I am free to regain the faith of a child.

When we, like children, see glimpses of the real world—where distance between people, the land, and the Creator is collapsed, where things like money or governments or class superiority are understood to be collaborative lies—we are getting close to the practice of *naming*.

Radical educator Paulo Freire suggests that naming is the heart of what it means to be authentically human:

> To exist, humanly, is to *name* the world, to change it. Once named, the world in its turn reappears to the namers as a problem and requires of them a new *naming* . . . But while to say the true word— which is work, which is praxis—is to transform the world, saying that word is not the privilege of some few persons, but the right of everyone. Consequently, no one can say a true word alone—nor can she say it *for* another, in a prescriptive act which robs others of their words . . . The naming of the world, which is an act of creation and re-creation, is not possible if it is not infused with love.[5]

What does this naming look like? It is noticing when members of the dominant culture are the only ones speaking in a mixed group and pointing it out. It is confessing those times when we've dismissed people because of our unrecognized prejudices. It is acknowledging the dignity and beauty of those experiencing injustice. It is standing with societal cast-offs while denouncing the systems that disregard them.

Naming happens whenever truth is spoken in the face of untruth and is acted upon. It is risky.

Naming happens when we bring hidden things to light, speak truth in the midst of error, or confess our complicity with systems that devalue others. Naming is about exposing the lies, and binding ourselves to reality with our attentiveness, presence, words, and actions. We are moving beyond mere symbolism to real praxis—acting in a way that unveils the oppression and co-creates liberation.

For example, we once had a man, "Malcolm," apply for long-term residence at the Mennonite Worker. Before a new housemate moves into one of our community houses, the members of the community have to reach

---

4. Sölle, *Silent Cry*, 13.

5. Freire, *Pedagogy of the Oppressed*, 69–70.

consensus. In this particular case, it took us months to reach consensus. Since Malcolm was in his sixties, had significant health issues, and has disabilities, we reached a unanimous decision to reject his application. A process that lasted months was finally over.

All that week, I felt troubled by the decision. So much prayer and discussion had been involved and we had at last reached consensus (those of you who have engaged in consensus decision-making understand how difficult it can be). Yet, I felt like we had made a mistake. I felt as though our decision had been driven by anxiety, rather than being based upon the leading of the Spirit. And so, one week after reaching full consensus, I awkwardly monkeywrenched the endeavor.

"I know we reached consensus . . . so I can't block consensus anymore, but if I could go back to last week and do so, I would," I said while avoiding eye contact with members of the community. I went on to explain how I felt I had been making decisions based upon anxiety and that I hadn't completely valued what Malcolm brought to our community—I'd become fixated on his age and health and disabilities. I was, in other words, making decisions like an anxious snob, and I suspected that the Spirit might be saying something different.

The reaction surprised me: I heard sighs of relief. Within ten minutes we reached consensus to overturn a decision that had taken months to make. I named my anxiety. I named my ageism and ableism. By bringing these hidden things to light, we were able to include someone who would otherwise be excluded. And, as a result, not only was Malcolm's life changed, ours was as well.

Naming is what Jesus is doing in the Sermon on the Mount. In the Beatitudes, Jesus is naming the truth and opening the space for a new reality in that naming. Were the poor blessed before Jesus said, "Blessed are the poor"? Were they, as we've assumed, blessed because of their awareness of need? Was Jesus sentimentalizing? Or was he, in that moment of naming, unveiling the lies and, with his fellow poor, co-creating a new reality? A new moment when previously entrenched realities break open so that a new future is possible? This is revolution-speak.

In the existing order, the wealthy and powerful and privileged were insiders. The poor were outsiders. In the Sermon on the Mount, Jesus flipped the social arrangement by naming the excluded as part of the Blessed. It was, in effect, like saying, "We don't need that system of power and exclusion. Here and now, *we* can be the community God desires."

Naming is about the in-breaking of God. When we speak the truth in the midst of a system of lies, the truth has been planted like a seed. And as we continue naming that truth begins to grow. In the Christian tradition, naming is almost the same thing as proclaiming the Gospel.

Later, on our way home, I wanted Jonas to tell Mommy what he had told me at the fountain. I'm one of those parents who likes to show off the intelligence of their kid. Unfortunately, Jonas never repeats himself; I can never get him to repeat his clever stories or phrases. I think Jonas enjoys subverting me.

"Jonas," I asked, "is Jesus alive?"

This time, he answered, "Jesus is everywhere . . . but he is alive in our hearts."

"But earlier, you said he was dead in the cities and buildings and in the outside!" I retorted.

He replied, "He is dead in those places because Herod tried to kill him and the bad people killed him and put him on a cross."

Jonas sees no contradiction between Jesus being dead in some places but alive everywhere. Of course, this isn't a rational idea, but it is, perhaps, a true one. In every moment, in every place, it is possible to encounter God—to see the world made new, to name the truth and push back lies. But it is also true that there are places and moments of de-creation—where death reigns.

I'm reminded of Óscar Romero's statement that "Christ is being crucified in his people." Where oppression reigns, people experience death. But where oppression reigns, Christ is suffering with the people. And where Christ encounters death, there is the possibility of resurrection.

Jesus is dead in the places we kill him. But he lives in our hearts. In each moment we're pulled in two directions—to continue to live in the broken world-as-it-is or to name the world, re-creating it as the kingdom of God breaks in.

In this way, the Great Commission, "go and make disciples of all nations," is a mandate for naming. The Great Commission can be seen as a top-down task of proselytizing or expanding Christendom. Or it can be seen as a bottom-up task of liberation. I am reminded of these stirring words by the immensely underappreciated William Stringfellow:

The premise of most urban church work, it seems, is that in order for the Church to minister among the poor, the Church has to be rich, that is, to have specially trained personnel, huge budgets, many facilities, rummage to distribute, and a whole battery of social services. Rather, the opposite is the case. The Church must be free to be poor in order to minister among the poor. The Church must trust the Gospel enough to come among the poor with nothing to offer the poor except the Gospel, except the power to discern and the courage to expose the Gospel as it is already mediated in the life of the poor . . . When the Church has the freedom itself to be poor among the poor, it will know how to use what riches it has. When the Church has that freedom, it will know also how to minister among the rich and powerful. When the Church has that freedom, it will be a missionary people again in all the world.[6]

The kingdom of God breaks into our reality through the lives of the seemingly insignificant. In small acts. In true words. We don't experience God's presence in the places of power or wealth or prestige. The kingdom comes to us in the unexpected places.

It won't begin unless it begins within us. Jesus is everywhere . . . his presence in-breaks and sustains. But he is dead in the places where he isn't animated by the hearts of his people. We cannot make true in the world what isn't true with us. Let us reclaim the imagination of children. And enter the kingdom. Let us show the world Jesus' impossible vision.

6. Stringfellow, *Private and Public Faith*, 80.

CHAPTER FOUR GROUP GUIDE

🗣 Summary

Children live in worlds as large as their imagination. And, unfortunately, so do adults. Our problem is not simply that our world is a broken place. Our problem is also that we live in too small a world, where our imaginations cannot see a way forward. We accept "what is" all too readily. We are called to see the world differently and to name new possibilities.

💬 Discussion Questions

1. The author writes, "Naming happens whenever truth is spoken in the face of untruth and is acted upon." When have you experienced something like this?

2. Read the Beatitudes in Matthew 5:3–12. Which of Jesus' statements are the hardest to believe?

3. The author writes that mysticism is about "encountering the living God wherever God may be. Mysticism collapses the distance between a person and God, between people, and between a person and the rest of creation. At its best, mysticism points toward a life free from abstraction, where you simply see what is." Can you share an example of this from your life?

✗ Group Practice: Centering Prayer

- Centering Prayer is a method of contemplative prayer used by Christians that emphasizes inner silence. It is a powerful practice that has helped many begin to grow in their capacity to give attention to themselves, to God, and to the rest of creation.

- Choose a sacred word to focus your attention. It might be a word from the Christian tradition like *Jesus, Mary, Abba, Mercy,* or *Love.* But really any word is fine. This isn't like using a mantra; the goal of Centering Prayer is to use the word to anchor your attention when you find it drifting to anxieties or concerns or other busy thoughts.

- For up to thirty minutes, sit in silence. When thoughts or feelings come into your awareness, simply recognize them and then inwardly say the sacred word. Rather than repeating the word mechanically, repeat the word like a prayer. Recognize that you are inwardly saying the word in the presence of God.

- When thoughts or emotions arise, bring the mind back to the sacred word.

- For people new to this practice—but also for those of us who have practiced Centering Prayer for years—it can be challenging. Remember: there isn't a wrong way to do Centering Prayer. The Spirit is present whether or not you recognize the Spirit.

🕯 Close with a time of silence or prayer.

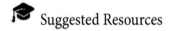 Suggested Resources

The Big Book of Christian Mysticism, by Carl McColman
The Silent Cry: Mysticism and Resistance, by Dorothee Sölle

Manifesto (Luke 4:18–19)

Drawing in the hot breath of God,
my shaking lungs sting
struggling to contain the power of the Almighty.
So I exhale the God-breath
upon those awaiting salvation,
prophesying powerful portents of liberation,
awakening the imaginations of the dispossessed.

This is my manifesto:

"This is your day, pauper.
Your empty stomachs will be filled with justice.
Your lean pockets will burst with peace.
The Heavenly Banker stocks your account
with cash stolen from the money changers.
No more hanging your head low.
No more thrift store spirituality.
You are the princes of the Kingdom.

Freedom is yours, prisoner.
Your cell bars will turn to noodles.
You'll exchange the dank dark for golden sunsets.
The New Warden has signed your parole papers
and put the old wardens behind bars.
No more scratching the days into brick walls.
No more false religion shutting out the stars.
Now you sleep under the rising red moon.

Open your eyes, blind man.
The darkness will be choked by light,
confusion broken by the sound of a trumpet.
The Holy Physician shows you a new world
while the watchmen are lost in the fog.
No more rubbing your eyes in despair.
No more stumbling in perpetual night.
You will bear witness to the edges of the world.

Step out of the shadows, oppressed.
The Principalities will lose their thrones.
The Powers will fall to earth.
The Spirit of God has ended this occupation
while the imperial fleet burns to ash and floats away.
No more plotting impotent rebellions.
No more struggling against steel and flesh.
For you are free citizens of a new nation.

The old fire has been suffocated
while holy coals smolder,
purifying the hearts of the people.
I announce the jubilee upon those shivering in fear,
shouting a sermon of shalom
as dawn of the first day breaks upon those He loves."

5

Hearing the Gospel of the unKingdom

> This holy anarchist who summoned the people at the bottom, the outcasts and "sinners," the chandalas within Judaism, to opposition against the dominant order . . . was a political criminal . . . This brought him to the cross.
>
> —FRIEDRICH NIETZSCHE

TRADITIONALLY, SCRIPTURE HAS BEEN used as an authoritarian text to justify the powerful. Today, we see a dominant form of Christianity wielding Scripture to animate nationalism, to exclude and condemn whole swathes of people.

However, as we see in the gospels, Christ's kingship is inconsistent with traditional structures of power—and for this reason, Jesus tells Pilate, "My kingdom is not from this world" (John 18:36). Passages like this have, unfortunately, fostered an ineffectual otherworldliness among Christians. And they have been used to legitimate "real-world" kingdoms. Jesus rules some magical sky-kingdom, while princes and emperors can dominate flesh and land.

Traditional kingship (with absolute power, hoarding of wealth, and power over the weak) has nothing to do with Jesus; it's something Jesus rejected.[1]

---

1. See John 6:15.

Traditional kings demand allegiance and servitude, but Jesus offers liberation—from suffering, sickness and death, exclusion, persecution, and sin. Jesus is a "king" who serves "the least of these" and who finally suffers torture and execution to bring freedom to others.

But Jesus' reign isn't otherworldly. It isn't apolitical. It's just political in a radically different way. Rather than taking Caesar's throne (or any throne—including the one offered to him by Satan)[2] Jesus is saying that Caesar's days are numbered. By saying "My kingdom is not from this world" he isn't saying "My kingdom is only spiritual, so you don't have to worry." A number of scholars have successfully made this point. For example, N. T. Wright argues, "The sentence should not be read as referring to an other-worldly, Platonic, non-physical kingdom. It designates Jesus' kingdom as the breaking into the worldly order of a rule which comes from elsewhere, from Israel's God, the creator God. It does not mean the abandonment of the created order and the escape into a private or 'spiritual' sphere. On to the scene of worldly power—precisely there, or it is meaningless!—has come a new order of sovereignty, which wins its victories by a new method."[3]

Jesus' kingship renders Caesar's obsolete. It isn't a mere "trumping," as though Jesus is simply *greater* than Caesar; it is an entirely different sort of kingship.

As heirs to Jesus' kingdom, we are ambassadors of the new reign, privileged to share the mercy, love, peace, and justice of Christ with the world. In the early days—the first century of the Jesus movement—the church was invisible to most people in the Roman Empire. However, the early Christians had a growing reputation as an alternative and seemingly antisocial community that lived in the nooks and crannies of Empire.

So, when Jesus said his kingdom is not from this world, he wasn't understood by Pilate or by the Jews or by his earliest followers as talking about the afterlife or some abstracted spiritual truth. Based upon the lethal response to Jesus (and the early reactions to Jesus' movement), the "kingdom of God" was understood as a challenge to Caesar and his reign. Their two kingdoms clashed.

The kingdom of God that Jesus announced and embodied is what life would be like on earth, here and now, if God were king and the rulers of this world were not. Imagine if God ruled the nations.

—

2. See Matt 4:1–11 and Luke 4:1–13.

3. Wright, "New Testament and the 'State,'" 11–17.

But in order to imagine that, we'd need to recognize that Jesus' kingdom isn't the sort that one holds tightly and controls with an iron fist. Despite our images of God, I'm not sure that God is interested in either hierarchy or control. For where the president of the United States insists on a troop surge, Jesus calls people to love their enemies. Where dictators seek to secure their own power and prestige, Jesus calls people to serve one another and lay down their lives for friends. Since Jesus is (as Christians believe) the truest revelation of God, he defines for us what the reign of God looks like.

The social, economic, political, and religious subversions of such an un-reign are almost endless—peace-making instead of warmongering, liberation not exploitation, sacrifice rather than subjugation, mercy not vengeance, care for the vulnerable instead of privilege for the powerful, generosity instead of greed, embrace rather than exclusion.

It is radically insufficient to simply say that Jesus' authority trumps other sorts of authority. This assumes that Jesus is just *more* kingly than earthly rulers, or that Jesus is just more powerful than the global elite. There is truth in this. But it is perhaps more apt to see Jesus' authority as so counter to earthly authority that it is, in fact, an un-authority. An authority to end authority. His power is a subversive power that tears down the elite. It tears down mountains and lifts up valleys.

Jesus is calling for a loving anarchy. An unKingdom. Of which he is the unking.[4]

NAMERS OF ALL FORMS OF OPPRESSION

Defining anarchism is problematic (to "define" something often implies the authority to do so, after all). Nevertheless, for the sake of clarity, I will offer my best attempt at a reasonable definition. "An-arch" means contrary to authority or without ruler. So "anarchism" is the name given to the idea that a group of people may live together without being ruled.

That is the textbook definition. Most anarchists go further, trying to name and resist all those things in our societies that oppress people. Elisabeth Schüssler Fiorenza coined the helpful term *kyriarchy* (from the Greek word *kyros*, which can signify the domination of the emperor, lord, master, father, husband, or elite propertied male) to signify the complex

---

4. A special thanks to my friend Jason Evans for teaching me the word *unking* as a way of describing Jesus.

interrelatedness of various forms of oppression (classism, sexism, hetero-normativity, racism, etc.). These various forms of domination do not stand alone. Rather, they reinforce one another into a domination system.[5]

I have found it helpful to focus my critique on Empire as a manifestation of interrelated oppressions. Empire is, in our context, that social reality (or unreality, depending on how you look at it) that globally reaches out to manage all of creation (including humanity) in a system of exploitation in which only the elite ultimately benefit.

Empire is the bringing of death to the whole of life. Good anarchists are namers of all forms of oppression, seeking to understand the way oppressions reinforce each other in enslaving creation and seeing, in contrast, a way of liberation and life for all of creation.

Anarchism is, as a defined idea, a new concept. This complicates any effort to delve too deeply into the past in order to name any group or movement as "anarchist." However, as anthropologist David Graeber writes,

> The basic principles of anarchism—self-organization, voluntary association, mutual aid—referred to forms of human behavior . . . [that] have been around about as long as humanity. The same goes for the rejection of the State and of all forms of structural violence, inequality, or domination . . . even the assumption that all these forms are somehow related and reinforce each other. None of it was presented as some startling new doctrine. And in fact it was not: one can find records of people making similar arguments throughout history, despite the fact there is every reason to believe that in most times and places, such opinions were the ones least likely to be written down. We are talking less about a body of theory, then, than about an attitude, or perhaps one might even say a faith: the rejection of certain types of social relations, the confidence that certain others would be much better ones on which to build a livable society, the belief that such a society could actually exist.[6]

It would make sense for those who follow Jesus Christ (who presumably want to embody the way of love) would feel drawn to a set of practices that seek to remove oppressive social relations and, instead, seek a new way of relating. Christians can learn from anarchists.

---

5. For more on this, see Schüssler Fiorenza's *Power of the Word: Scripture and the Rhetoric of Empire.*

6. Graeber, *Fragments,* 3–4.

ANARCHIC IMPULSES IN SCRIPTURE

A superficial reading of the Bible reveals a God who thinks of *him*self as a sort of Warrior King who sanctions state-enacted genocide and who promotes a string of saintly kings, like King David. Many Christians assume that when Jesus arrives, it is to initiate a kingdom of God that, apparently, seems content to coexist with earthly rulership. They hear Jesus saying "Render to Caesar what is Caesar's" and Paul advocating being good subjects to the governing authorities. Therefore, Christian anarchism can be seen as a contradiction in terms.

Furthermore, how can Christian anarchists hold views like nonviolence when many biblical heroes were prolific smiters? How can Christian anarchists support communal ownership when certain patriarchs were "blessed" with vast property—which they didn't share equally with all? How can Christian anarchists argue for consensus decision-making when Paul tends to affirm male leadership and Jesus praises a centurion who holds a position of authority? To many people, the last thing the Bible offers is an anarchist perspective.

I think there is a different way to read Scripture. There is an anarchic impulse running throughout Scripture that, once you find it, begins to subvert many conventional interpretations.

The Hebrew Scriptures

Let's start at the beginning. Genesis can be read as an anti-civilizational text. It begins with the story of humans living in harmony with nature and upholds that as a pristine ideal. As Ched Myers suggests,

> In the "primeval history" of Gen 1–11 Israel's sages—redacting older sources and probably writing in the aftermath of the failed monarchy—also attempted to explain [the rupture from primal life]. Eden can be interpreted as a mythic memory of the old symbiotic lifeways: humans, creatures and God dwell intimately and richly together (Gen 2).[7]

When paradise is lost, humans are relegated to hard agricultural toil.

The first act of violence is committed by the agriculturalist (Cain) rather than the nomadic herdsman (Abel). It is this murderer who establishes the first city. Later, as humanity "progresses," all sorts of crazy things

7. Myers, "Fall."

happen: the human population spikes, the "sons of *Elohim*" have sex with women, people become increasingly wicked, and God sends a flood to re-boot creation. Later, when folks gather to build a huge tower that reaches to the heavens, God scatters the people. For the most part, Genesis is re-markably negative about the way wickedness increases with the march of civilization.

Again, Myers writes,

> The "Fall" in Gen 1–11, then, is not so much a cosmic moment of moral failure as it is a progressive "history" of decline into civilization—exactly contrary to the Myth of Progress. The bibli-cal primeval history thus should be considered not only as "mythic memory," but also perhaps the first literature of resistance to the grand project of civilization—rightly warning against its social pathologies and ecocidal consequences.[8]

The rest of Genesis follows the story of the first patriarchs, whom YHWH has called out to become a people who will follow YHWH into a promised land. Throughout Genesis, trouble happens when the Jews favor-ably interact with imperial powers or try to settle too soon. While it is true that the patriarchs had many possessions, it is a stretch to infer from their wealth modern notions of property rights. Pre-agricultural nomadic peo-ples were tribal. While the patriarchs were hardly egalitarian, their under-standing of ownership was much more communal than modern Western notions. The wealth of the tribe or clan or family was for the benefit of all.

Exodus tells the story of a people enslaved by the Egyptian Empire and how YHWH delivers them. You know the story: YHWH calls Moses (in the burning bush theophany) to lead the Israelites out of slavery into a promised land. Of course, once liberated, the people grumble and com-plain—desiring a return to Egypt instead of the long journey in the wilder-ness. In Exodus, we see a "story of Israel's communal bonding around the mountain at which they encounter YHWH, with no need for 'sacrifice' of animals or enemies."[9] As a result of their grumbling, YHWH keeps them in the wilderness for forty years.

Then, apparently, Moses passes the mantle of leadership to Joshua—a sort of military hero who engages in war against the indigenous peoples of Canaan. The people successfully settle and are attacked by their neighbors,

8. Myers, "Fall," 636.

9. Howard-Brook, *"Come Out, My People!,"* 196.

leading YHWH to raise up "judges" to lead the people in combat against the enemies of Israel.

YHWH sets up a brilliant economic policy centered around the Sabbath. Every seven days is to be a day of rest, every seven years a time for the land to rest, and every seven times seven years the Jubilee, when all slaves were set free, every debt was released, and even the land reverted back to its ancestral ownership. It was an economic system that condemned usury, struck at the root of generational poverty, and condemned the exploitation of foreigners.

YHWH also instituted a strange political system; instead of having a centralized government, temporary leaders were called as need arose. God dwelled among the people to rule directly rather than ruling through kings or priests. For example, one of the leaders who emerges, Gideon, tells the people, "I will not rule over you, nor will my son rule over you. The LORD will rule over you."[10] Unfortunately, Gideon's offspring attempt to set up a dynasty.

But the people complained for a king, and eventually YHWH relented. Saul—who fits the people's idea of a king—was a failure. After he died in battle, David (after some oft-told Bible stories transpire) became king. The kingdom split during the time of David's grandson. Conflicts between the prophets and the kings became commonplace as Israel increasingly came to resemble its neighbors, leading to the eventual demise and captivity of both the northern and southern kingdoms.

This story—from Exodus to the monarchy—is one of centralization and waywardness. As Wes Howard-Brook writes,

> As it stands in its canonical order, the story conveys a relatively (and deceivingly) simple message: the shift from a twelve tribe confederacy under YHWH's rule to a human monarchy "like the nations" (1 Sam 8:5) was a disastrous betrayal of the unique status of Israel as YHWH's "chosen people" . . . Israel "converted" from a religion of creation to the religion of empire, with predictable results.[11]

It is important to highlight some of what makes this a "deceivingly" simple message. It is simplistic (and foolish) to assume that the days of David and Solomon, with a monarchy centralized in Jerusalem and worship centralized in a temple in Zion, should be considered a golden age.

---

10. Judg 8:23.

11. Howard-Brook, *"Come Out, My People!,"* 95.

There is, according to Howard-Brook, a tension (or outright contradiction) between the pro-monarchic "'Zion theology' that placed YHWH in the Jerusalem temple," where Solomon "could be understood as truly empowered by YHWH with 'wisdom,'" and the prophetic "Sinai theology" where "Solomon's 'experience' can be written off as either wishful thinking or simply as propaganda."[12]

In other words, the Hebrew Scriptures present a sort of argument between the religion of Empire (in which a faithful, powerful, secure, wealthy, and vast nation is centralized in Jerusalem, where YHWH and king dwell) and the religion of creation (in which a faithful people live in Jubilee, encounter YHWH in creation and amidst people, and live as kin without an earthly ruler).

As we read through the prophets, when God speaks, it is usually through a prophet who challenges the king's power and who stands outside of the machinations of the monarchy. The emphases of the kings are very different from those of the prophets. It is astonishing how much the prophets link idolatry and exploitation of the poor. The kings often centralize wealth and power. The prophets challenge that trend. The prophets, it would seem, still hold God's Jubilee vision in their imaginations.

Ezekiel points to a time when things will return to YHWH's original intent: God judges the "shepherds" or rulers of Israel, essentially striking them down to become the people's sole Shepherd:

> This is what the Sovereign LORD says: I am against the shepherds and will hold them accountable for my flock. I will remove them from tending the flock so that the shepherds can no longer feed themselves. I will rescue my flock from their mouths, and it will no longer be food for them . . . I myself will search for my sheep and look after them . . . I will search for the lost and bring back the strays. I will bind up the injured and strengthen the weak, but the sleek and the strong I will destroy. I will shepherd the flock with justice. (Ezek 34:10–11, 16)

The New Testament

If Wes Howard-Brook is right about there being an argument in Scripture between the religion of Empire and the religion of creation, then Jesus clearly and consistently sides with the religion of creation.

12. Howard-Brook, *"Come Out, My People!,"* 132.

Jesus' mother, while Jesus was still in the womb, said the following words while filled with the Spirit:

> [God] has demonstrated power with [God's] arm;
> [God] has scattered those whose pride wells up from the sheer arrogance of their hearts.
> [God] has brought down the mighty from their thrones,
> and has lifted up those of lowly position;
> [God] has filled the hungry with good things,
> and has sent the rich away empty. (Luke 1:51–53)

Jesus grows up. He starts his ministry and is tempted by the devil in the wilderness. The temptation of Jesus by the devil reveals the manner in which Jesus understands his authority. Jesus' sense of authority bears little to no similarity to kingly authority. In the wilderness, he is tempted politically, economically, and religiously to assert his messiahship. But he refuses. The diabolical nature of his temptation isn't due to the source of the temptation—that the offer of political, economic, and religious power comes from the devil instead of God. Rather, the temptation concerns the sort of reign Jesus should pursue. Jesus is the unking.

Later, in Luke 4, right after his trial and baptism, Jesus goes to his hometown (Nazareth) and gives a political manifesto of liberation for the poor and oppressed, essentially announcing his messiahship and the coming of Jubilee ("the year of the Lord's favor"). Provocatively, Jesus seems willing to include oppressors in the kingdom. The context makes this clear. The miracles Jesus references in his sermon involve the healing of Gentiles. Furthermore, when quoting Isaiah 61, he omits the portion that speaks of "the year of the Lord's vengeance," which was understood to refer to vengeance against the Gentile oppressors of Israel. Which is why his hometown folks—who most likely knew him well—try to kill him.[13]

In Luke 17:21 Jesus quotes Leo Tolstoy:[14] "The kingdom of God is within you" (or among you). In this context, it seems to be a way of suggesting that the kingdom of God isn't a place, a demonstrative regime change, or a clear event. Rather, it is here. Now. Jesus didn't like the way the political

---

13. I often wonder if any of these folks had babysat him. After all, it is generally assumed that Mary ended up being a single mother at some point, putting more of the parenting burden on her. It would suck to have your childhood babysitter try to kill you.

14. Apologies for my nerdy anarchist joke. If you don't get it, it is probably for the best.

game was played, so he played a different sort of game altogether: one without winners and losers.

Later, when Jesus heard his friends arguing over their position in the pecking order in this kingdom, he tells them, "The kings of the Gentiles lord it over them; and those who exercise authority over them call themselves Benefactors. But you are not to be like that. Instead, the greatest among you should be like the youngest, and the one who rules like the one who serves" (Luke 22:25–26). Jesus is asking his friends to rethink everything they know about sociopolitical realities.

The next time you read the Gospel of Luke, try to read it through the lens of Jubilee—where the ones who have accumulated have to give up their wealth and the ones who have lost receive. Jesus tells the rich young ruler to sell everything and give it to the poor.[15] He says the same thing to his disciples, by the way.[16]

Luke isn't the only anarchist-friendly gospel; John is also pretty juicy. For example, Jesus calls Satan "the prince of the world" (see John 12:31; 14:30; 16:11)—which is likely a way of referring to the Roman Empire. Walter Wink's work explores this further. The word we translate as "world" is *cosmos*, which Wink establishes as meaning something closer to "Domination System" or "Empire."[17]

After the resurrection, we read of an account of civil disobedience in Acts 5. When the disciples are ordered by the authorities to stop their teaching, they answer, "We must obey God rather than any human authority" (v. 29). Here's what most people have been taught this means: "We must obey God rather than any human authority in those rare circumstances where there is a clear and obvious contradiction between what the law says and God says, since God's laws trump human laws." I'm not so sure. If you believed that your messiah was a sociopolitical/religious unking who died and then rose from the dead (and then mystically poured his Spirit out upon you), then you might simply mean "We must obey God, not any human authority."

This helps us understand the way in which the early church practiced community. They were encouraged, among other things, to work out their

15. Luke 18:18–30.

16. Luke 12:13–34 is one of the most compelling economic passages in the entire Bible. I reference it here because many people assume that the call to redistribute wealth to the poor is made only to the rich young ruler in Luke 18. It is a more common theme than that, particularly in Luke's gospel.

17. See Wink's *Engaging the Powers*.

issues internally rather than appealing to the courts.[18] In Romans 12, Paul argues that his friends in Rome should "not be conformed to this present world [read: empire], but be transformed by the renewing of your mind, so that you may test and approve what is the will of God" (v. 2). This is often read as a call to be spiritually minded. But, given the larger context, it is perhaps better to see it as a challenge to stop being so Roman-ish and instead pursue the way of love. I am often asked to justify my anti-imperial reading of the New Testament. After all, the word *empire* doesn't appear in the New Testament. Well, here's the thing: the early church was sneaky. They didn't want to sound overtly treasonous. So, usually, we have to try to inhabit their context with our imaginations to see Rome closer to the way they saw it. And no writing is as anti-imperial, perhaps, as John's Revelation.

The "Babylon" referred to throughout Revelation was Rome; the ancient seat of imperial power during the days of exile (Babylon) came to signify the current imperial power. As Wes Howard-Brook and Anthony Gwyther argue, Revelation isn't a challenge to Roman imperialism, in particular, but to imperialism in general. Rome was the face of an old enemy.[19]

Babylon is described as "a dwelling of demons and a haunt for every evil spirit . . . For all the nations have drunk the maddening wine of her adulteries. The kings of the earth committed adultery with her, and the merchants of the earth grew rich from her excessive luxuries" (Rev 18:2–3). In response to imperialism, a voice from heaven declares, "Come out of her, my people, so that you will not share in her sins" (Rev 18:4b).

BUT WHAT ABOUT . . . ?

Yeah. I know. There are still a lot of open questions. My point here isn't so much to defend an anarchic read of Scripture as much as it is to give a sketch of the possibilities. We read Scripture in ways that support authoritarianism because we learned how to read Scripture in authoritarian contexts. Once you start pulling the loose threads, you begin to find the whole authoritarian fabric unraveling. For the sake of brevity, I'll address the two passages most commonly cited as evidence against Christian anarchism.

18. 1 Cor 6:1–6.

19. Howard-Brook and Gwyther, *Unveiling Empire.*

What about "Submit to the Governing Authorities"?

The first is Romans 13, where Paul tells his readers to "submit to the governing authorities":

> Let everyone be subject to the governing authorities, for there is no authority except that which God has established. The authorities that exist have been established by God. Consequently, whoever rebels against the authority is rebelling against what God has instituted, and those who do so will bring judgment on themselves. For rulers hold no terror for those who do right, but for those who do wrong. Do you want to be free from fear of the one in authority? Then do what is right and you will be commended. For the one in authority is God's servant for your good. But if you do wrong, be afraid, for rulers do not bear the sword for no reason. They are God's servants, agents of wrath to bring punishment on the wrongdoer. Therefore, it is necessary to submit to the authorities, not only because of possible punishment but also as a matter of conscience. This is also why you pay taxes, for the authorities are God's servants, who give their full time to governing. Give to everyone what you owe: If you owe taxes, pay taxes; if revenue, then revenue; if respect, then respect; if honor, then honor. (Rom 13:1–7)

When interpreting this passage, there are several things that one must keep in mind. This passage comes immediately after Romans 12, where Paul challenges his readers to bless persecutors, live peaceably, never avenge, feed enemies, and overcome evil with good. By implication, the "governing authorities" are persecuting enemies whose evil needs to be overcome with good. Given that Paul is likely drawing directly from Jesus' teachings, it may be best to interpret the call to "be subject" as an application of the call to "turn the other cheek." It is not a call to mere obedience or happy citizenship.

Not only is the passage a call to turn the other cheek, it is also a recognition that the conventional wisdom would be to strike back. Jacques Ellul suggests that "the passage thus counsels nonrevolution, but in so doing, by that very fact, it also teaches the intrinsic nonlegitimacy of institutions."[20] In other words, the very fact that Paul has to argue, in light of enemy-love, that the people should forsake (violent) resistance reveals that the "governing authorities" are, in some sense, worthy of revolt, just as Jesus' call to turn

---

20. Ellul, *Anarchy and Christianity*, 88.

the other cheek recognizes that, under normal circumstances, one would hit back. To refrain from violence is a testimony to the Roman Christians' goodness, not the goodness of Rome.

The admonition to "be subject" is offered because "the authorities that exist have been established by God." The word translated as "established" (or in other translations as "ordained" or "instituted") would seem to argue for a divine ordinance of governmental authority. However, John Howard Yoder has (rightly) challenged translating the Greek word *tetagmenai* (from the verb *tasso*) in any of these ways. Rather, Yoder argues that a better translation would be that the authorities are ordered or "put in line" by God. Therefore, Paul could be advising his readers against revolt since God is already dealing with the rulers.[21]

It is also important to note the way in which a substantial cultural gap plays in any treatment of this passage. The word translated in this passage as "authorities" or "authority" is *exousia*. Due to the nature of translation and the dualism in our modern imaginations (separating spiritual from political realms), we don't often recognize that Paul's use of the word *exousia* blurs the distinction between political and spiritual realities. See some of the ways the word is translated in other passages attributed to Paul:

> 1 Corinthians 15:24: "Then the end will come, when he hands over the kingdom to God the Father after he has destroyed all dominion, *authority* and power."
>
> Ephesians 1:19b–21: "That power is the same as the mighty strength he exerted when he raised Christ from the dead and seated him at his right hand in the heavenly realms, far above all rule and *authority*, power and dominion, and every name that is invoked, not only in the present age but also in the one to come."
>
> Ephesians 6:12: "For our struggle is not against flesh and blood, but against the rulers, against the *authorities*, against the powers of this dark world and against the spiritual forces of evil in the heavenly realms."
>
> Colossians 2:15: "And having disarmed the powers and *authorities*, he made a public spectacle of them, triumphing over them by the cross."

When we read words like "authorities" or "rulers" or "powers," Paul may be talking primarily about spiritual realities, political realities, or perhaps both at the same time. This adds complexity to what would otherwise seem like a straightforward challenge to be "subject" to the

---

21. See chapter 10 of John Howard Yoder's *Politics of Jesus*.

"authorities" because, elsewhere, such "authorities" are seen as enemies to Christ.

Finally, it is a mistake to take Romans 13 as a universal message of how Christians everywhere ought to relate to government. Wes Howard-Brook states,

> We can say, though, that whatever Paul meant to convey to the Christians at Rome in the 50s, it was not a general principle of subservience to imperial authority . . . We've seen how Paul's letters regularly insist on attributing to Jesus titles and authority that his audience would certainly have heard as "plagiarized" from Roman sources . . . The most likely explanation of Romans 13 is that it was a message addressed to specific concerns of Roman Christians under Nero.[22]

And so, from Paul's perspective, the Christians in Rome in the 50s should not revolt. Rather, they should love their oppressors and leave wrath to God. This wasn't because the Roman government was good but because followers of Jesus are called to the way of love. Furthermore, God has put the authorities in line and will judge them.

Much could be said about what Romans 13 could mean for us. At the very least, it encourages us to trust God and love our enemies. While Paul argues against violent resistance, his words leave room for nonviolent struggle. It would be foolish, I think, to extrapolate universal principles of governmental engagement from this passage. Nevertheless, once we understand Paul's sentiments, we can better discern how to express the love of God in our own contexts.

What about "Render unto Caesar?"

Tied for the most referenced anti-anarchy passage is Mark 12:13–17:

> Later they sent some of the Pharisees and Herodians to Jesus to catch him in his words. They came to him and said, "Teacher, we know that you are a man of integrity. You aren't swayed by others, because you pay no attention to who they are; but you teach the way of God in accordance with the truth. Is it right to pay the imperial tax to Caesar or not? Should we pay or shouldn't we?
>
> But Jesus knew their hypocrisy. "Why are you trying to trap me?" he asked. "Bring me a denarius and let me look at it." They

22. Howard-Brook, *"Come Out, My People!,"* 464.

brought the coin, and he asked them, "Whose image is this? And whose inscription?"

"Caesar's," they replied.

Then Jesus said to them, "Give back to Caesar what is Caesar's and to God what is God's." And they were amazed at him.

Clearly, they were trying to trick Jesus into publicly picking sides—either would be dangerous. If he sided with Rome, he'd lose the support of the people. If he denounced Rome, he'd be a marked man. The fact that Herodians and Pharisees are working together against Jesus is noteworthy; Jesus was enough of a threat to cause two rival factions to join forces.

Are the implications that we should create a distinction between church and state? Or even separate them into two separate kingdoms with different claims as Luther or some Anabaptists have advocated? No. This is a very smart slap against Caesar without simply denouncing Caesar. By pointing to their coin (no good Jew should have a graven image like a coin in their pocket to begin with), Jesus is exposing idolatry and saying that such things belong to Caesar already, not God. If you've got any Caesar-stuff, it should be rendered accordingly. But what is God's belongs to God. Or, to quote Dorothy Day, "If we rendered unto God all the things that belong to God, there would be nothing left for Caesar."

Lest you think that such approaches to Scripture are a recent innovation, I direct you to Irenaeus. Irenaeus was a second-century bishop on the fringes of the Empire in Lugdunum, Gaul. He was a disciple of Polycarp, who was a disciple of the Apostle John. In other words, he was removed from Jesus by two generations; he was a friend of a friend of Jesus:

> The Lord himself directed us to "render unto Caesar the things that are Caesar's, and to God the things that are God's"; naming indeed Caesar as Caesar, but confessing God as God. In like manner also, that [text] which says, "You cannot serve two masters," he does himself interpret, saying, "You cannot serve God and mammon"; acknowledging God indeed as God, but mentioning mammon, a thing having also an existence. He does not call mammon Lord when he says, "You cannot serve two masters"; but he teaches his disciples who serve God, not to be subject to mammon, nor to be ruled by it.[23]

23. Irenaeus, *Against Heresies*, 3.8.1 (*ANF* 1:421).

In other words, Irenaeus believed that the thing we should render to Caesar is our renunciation. Caesar's lordship is comparable to that of mammon.[24] He is only your lord if you are his slave.

My hope in offering this quick overview of the Scriptures is not to satisfy every troubling question. Rather, I've shown the rough contours of a lens: a lens that forswears Empire and, instead, opts for liberation for all people. My intention is not to offer a novel reading of Scripture but to draw attention to themes that have been there all along, buried under centuries of theological justification.

The remainder of this book is my attempt at answering, "So now what?"

---

24. Mammon is more than mere "money." It is likely that Jesus (and the early church) thought of Mammon as something demonic. "Mammon" signified not only money or wealth but also the entire economic system of exploitation. By the Middle Ages, many conceived of Mammon as the arch-demon of greed.

CHAPTER FIVE GROUP GUIDE

 Summary

The Bible is conventionally understood as an authoritarian text. However, there is an "anarchic" impulse throughout Scripture that finds its fullest expression in the life and teachings of Jesus.

Discussion Questions

1. What do you think of the author's summary of the "anarchist" impulses within Scripture? What questions or concerns stir within you when you look at Scripture as an antiauthoritarian text?

2. In what ways have you experienced Scripture used as a tool for control and domination? In what ways have you experienced Scripture used as a source of liberation?

3. What would it look like to take seriously the Jesus described in this chapter?

Group Practice

- Return to the large sheets of paper from your discussion of chapter 1. What would you add to each sheet of paper? What would you change?

- Give ten to fifteen minutes for journaling. Ask each member of your group to answer this question: Where do I, personally, feel the biggest tension between the conventional wisdom of our society and the teachings of Jesus? Ask everyone to share as much as they are comfortable.

Close with a time of silence or prayer.

Suggested Resources

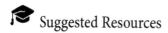

The Biblical Jubilee and the Struggle for Life, by Ross and Gloria Kinsler
"Come Out, My People!", by Wes Howard-Brook
Jesus and the Disinherited, by Howard Thurman

ELDER TREE

In dark morning
still and cool
I go where the great rivers meet.
I place my hand on the elder tree.
My fragile skin rubs the rough bark.
My soul leeches from flesh to wood
and slides down into the roots
where soil and blood mingle.
I am planted there with that elder tree;
it remembers, so I remember.
We share mysteries from beneath,
under the wet grass.
Rooted, I am free
to reject those old lies
and drink deeply of older truths.
I remember a time before the great forgetting
when all were wild and free.
I lift my arms to tickle the wind,
the spirit blowing through my fingertips.
From root to tip
I begin to dance.

6

Encountering the Feral God

Jesus is dead in the buildings and in the cities and in the outside. But he is alive in our hearts.

—St. Jonas of Minneapolis

Ours is a civilized god. He is distant, floating high above the world, refusing to be dirtied by it. He is the Supreme Hierarch, the Ruler of All. The Great Architect, looking down over all of creation and ordering it according to his Divine Blueprint. Of all of the things he's created, he likes human beings the best. Sometimes he communicates to some of these humans, revealing to them part of his Divine Blueprint. Our primary relationship with this god is one of obedience; we are to do his will so that things can work according to the Blueprint.

This god works well with imperialism. Imperialism is about ordering creation. It is about obedience. It is about mastery. This god is the creation of an imperial imagination.

The god we have shaped in our image has re-created humanity. We too live above the world, separate from it. As abstracted from it as our god is from us. We live in a world of distances—where humanity is separated from God, where person is alienated from person, and where we have forsaken our creatureliness to rule creation. Ours is a lonely world.

In order to make sense of our chaotic, lonely world, we create blueprints of our own and try to control what is around us to conform it to that blueprint. We do this because we worship a blueprinting god. Insofar as we worship this god-with-a-blueprint whose first requirement is obedience (understood in its traditional, monological sense), we place ourselves in a story of imperialism.

Some may balk at this. Many Christians, after all, have found a way to worship a god who demands obedience while, at the same time, living in ways of mutuality, love, and humility in their own lives. Nevertheless, I suspect there is an unresolved tension within their minds and hearts: why, they may ask, does this god act in one way and then call me to another? In the end, they accept some sort of Divine Exceptionalism. Much like the United States (or any other empire) holds itself to a different standard than subordinate nations, so too this god can commit acts of genocide, violence, and oppression while (without any sense of irony) telling us to love our enemies, turn the other cheek, and practice mutual submission. It is one step from worshiping such an exceptional god to embracing imperialism in his name.

Before I go further, I want to clarify a bit what I'm getting at when I say "obedience." I'm not encouraging divine disobedience (not exactly). Rather, I'm advocating for a reimagining of what obedience looks like. And a reimagining of our image of God. I believe God's concern is primarily for us to be like Jesus, not simply to act like Jesus through obedience.

John 15 (where Jesus says, "I no longer call you servants") seems to point in a direction that challenges conventional notions of obedience. It is interesting that Jesus says, in the same breath, "I no longer call you servants" and "If you obey my command you are my friends." This seems kinda strange, until you examine the nature of the command: to love.

Here Jesus is offering an understanding of obedience that is different. It is no longer monological (I say and you do) but dialogical (we are now friends). Just as the lordship of Jesus subverts our notions of reign, so too does Jesus' call to obedience subvert our notions of obedience.

When you have a lord who undoes lordship and a master who subverts mastery, then everything is different. I think it is a mistake to assume that obedience to such a One is at all similar to other patterns of obedience.

This line of thought is hardly original. I first encountered such unsettling (and liberating) thoughts in the writings of Dorothee Sölle, who asks,

Can one demand a particular stance toward God and educate toward that stance, yet simultaneously criticize that same stance toward people and toward institutions? Is it actually possible, in the realities of daily life, to distinguish between the obedience which is due God and that obedience toward people which we can and ought with good reason refuse? I suspect that we Christians today have the duty to criticize the entire concept of obedience, and that this criticism must be radical, simply because we do not know exactly who God is and what God, at any given moment, wills. It is no longer possible to describe our relationship to God with a formal concept that is limited to the mere performance of duties. We cannot remove ourselves from history if we wish to speak seriously about God. And in our Christian history, our history of the 20th century, obedience has played a catastrophic role.[1]

Sölle isn't suggesting that we abandon obedience, as though we should rebel against God. Rather, she suggests a reexamination of obedience in light of Jesus' witness:

[Obedience] does not mean the carrying out of commands, and most assuredly not in the sense of Benedict's continually repeated decision to obey the abbot the way Christ obeyed God. Obedience means instead a decision which first discovers God's will in doing. The person herself must decide what is to be done; she is not the fulfiller of assigned commands. Nothing is here taken from the autonomy of the subject. The will of God does not represent external demands and it is not predetermined or fixed . . . It is not God in a general, timeless sense who demands obedience, but the situation which demands a response, and only therein does God require a person's response . . . an obedience which has its eyes wide open, which first discovers God's will in the situation, a discerning obedience.[2]

Our relationship with God shapes our relationship to one another and to the land. If that relationship is seen primarily as one of subjects to the Supreme Hierarch, our imaginations will tend toward imperialism.

Let me be practical. Even the most basic act—offering food to a stranger—can be radically different depending upon how it is held in our imaginations. Offering bread can be a condescending act of charity to those "less fortunate" or a step toward justice as bread is shared among equals

1. Sölle, *Beyond Mere Obedience*, 10.

2. Ibid., 24–25.

around the table of Jesus. From the outside, the act of offering food to a stranger may look the same, but its liberating potential is often determined by our hearts, and our hearts are often shaped by what we love the most. Jesus said, "Where your treasure is, there is your heart." The god we worship matters.

In the Hebrew Scriptures, whenever the people had been seduced by imperial images of God, the voices of the prophets would echo calls of repentance from the margins. As Wes Howard-Brook suggests, the prophetic voice calls us out of the religion of Empire to embrace the religion[3] of creation:

> We can understand one of the Bible's religions to be grounded in the *experience of and ongoing relationship with the Creator God,* leading to a covenantal bond between that God and God's people for the blessing and abundance of *all* people and *all* creation. The other, while sometimes *claiming* to be grounded in that same God, is actually a human invention used to justify and legitimate attitudes and behaviors that provide blessing and abundance for *some* at *the expense of others.*[4]

The prophets call us to worship the God who is the source of life, the giver of life. This God is a creative, feral spring from which our own lives pour. We encounter this God in the wild places, where life is unfettered. We encounter this God when we name and let go (repent) of those structures that trammel life and subjugate people and the land.

Ours is a world in need of prophets and mystics. The Hebrew prophets spoke from the wilderness, a place without cities and kings and temples. The wilderness is a place of creation—where a person is free to be a creature. It is a place where pretenses are stripped away, where the distances can collapse.

The prophets remind us that faith is not a tool of domination. Faith is a feral force that sets us free to love and encounter each other without a blueprint.

Howard-Brook writes, "Moses encountered YHWH outside of Egypt, outside of empire, in the *wilderness* and at a *mountain.* These two sites are

---

3. It is fashionable for Christians to reject "religion." Often this is largely a semantic game. In this context, I'm not using the word *religion* in a derogatory sense but in the broad way that Wes Howard-Brook defines it, drawing upon the Latin meaning of *religio,* "to bind again": "the attitudes, beliefs, and/or practices that bind individuals together as a 'people.'" Howard-Brook, *"Come Out, My People!,"* 5.

4. Ibid., 7.

the repeated places in which YHWH encounters Israel."[5] Moses meets God in the place free from civilization, apart from the city. Apart from the place of domination.

It is significant that before Jesus begins his ministry, he goes into the wild: "And at once the Spirit drove him into the desert and he remained there for forty days and was put to the test by Satan. He was with the wild animals, and the angels looked after him" (Mark 1:12–13).

Notice that, even though Jesus is "alone," he is not alone. The distance has collapsed. The Spirit has brought him to the wild place, where he is in fellowship with creation (with the wild animals), and even the veil of heaven is opened as he fellowships with the angels. Even Satan is present, to be confronted for what he is.

The wilderness is the place of unvarnished truth. I'm not suggesting that if we merely go into the woods, all truth will be revealed. Nor am I suggesting that being in a city necessarily taints us. Nevertheless, it is in the wilderness—the place of creatureliness—that Jesus encounters the world as it is. And he brings that feral faith with him all the way to the temple, where he confronts the religion of Empire.

The religion of Empire is presented by Satan—to use economic, political, and religious power to enforce the messianic agenda. But Jesus said no to three temptations and, angry at the devil, chose a different way.

The wilderness was the place where Jesus spoke the truth to Satan (the animating force of Empire) and became himself the path to liberation.

We need to rewild our faith, to reject our assumptions about religion and power and sustenance. Our most pressing need is to develop practices that help us see the world through a different lens than that of imperial myths and civilizational programming.

The feral faith of Jesus probably has more in common with traditional tribal spirituality than it does with what we think of as "Christianity." In the prophetic tradition, and in the experience of Jesus, the Feral God is found primarily in creation, not in a temple. This isn't to say that God is absent in holy buildings. But it is perhaps fair to say that God is present to us in spite of our holy accoutrements and machinations, rather than because of them.

5. Ibid., 143.

PRACTICES FOR ENCOUNTERING THE FERAL GOD

So, what does this rewilding look like? I want to be careful not to offer a list of things to fix our faith, as though offering a blueprint can fix our addiction to blueprints. However, I have found three practices to be useful in helping me encounter the Feral God. They aren't magical practices. But they can provide a way for us to encounter the Feral God.

Practice One: Experimenting with God

It is tragic that the way of Jesus has become a disembodied set of principles. We need to relearn the way of Jesus—not simply by rereading Scripture but by relearning how to see Scripture. Our challenge isn't in finding the right content but in reading things with the right eyes. How we learn is perhaps more important than what we learn. Most of us, I suspect, have learned quite a bit about Jesus but haven't been encouraged by our churches to learn from Jesus or to learn in the way Jesus taught. Because of this, we've treated our discipleship like a math class: crack open a book, learn the content, and hope (somehow) it will make (someday) a difference in our lives.

This approach is so entrenched that any attempt to practice the way of Jesus is seen as extreme. And, depending upon our political orientation, this extremity is either praised or ridiculed.

In 2003, my wife and I formed Missio Dei (which is now called the Mennonite Worker) with a simple premise; we would read the gospels and ask three questions as we read:

1. What is Jesus saying or doing in this passage?

2. What excuses are stirring in our minds as a way of justifying why we shouldn't do likewise?

3. What is at least one thing we can do to walk in the direction of what Jesus is saying or doing?

These questions eventually led my wife and me, and a handful of our friends, to form an intentional community that centered its life around the practice of hospitality. The approach was largely experimental; there were no preset notions of what it should look like to follow the way of Jesus. Nor were we trying to push ourselves to new heights of heroism. Rather, we challenged one another to be honest with our fears and recognize at least one step we could take.

My own spirit of experimentation deepened in subsequent years as I became friends with Mark Scandrette. His community in San Francisco had been engaging in an innovative (yet ancient) approach to learning the way of Jesus that Mark dubbed the "Jesus Dojo." The idea wasn't simply to experiment more deeply with the way of Jesus but to treat these experiments as a way of learning.

One experiment they did involved living into John the Baptist's command in Luke 3:11 that anyone who has two tunics should share with the one who has none. As a result, Mark and his friends decided to sell half of their possessions and give the money to the poor. This act wasn't treated as an end in itself. Rather, throughout the process they discussed with one another the thoughts and feelings that surfaced. The idea wasn't simply to help the poor but also to examine their own hearts and transform their relationship with material goods. Instead of assuming they had done a good deed by putting the teachings of Jesus into practice, they approached their divestment as a way of learning the way of Jesus.

The goal of an experimental faith isn't to "get things right." Such a way of seeing the world is static and lifeless. Rather, truth is dynamic and relational. It allows us to learn new things about ourselves and our God. It opens us to encounter the Feral God in our midst who shows us a new way. The goal isn't to obey abstract rules but to enter into a relationship with Jesus, to learn from Jesus, to become more like Jesus.

Practice Two: Embracing Our Creatureliness

If we want to encounter a wild God, we need to embrace our creatureliness. Just as Jesus linked love of God with love of neighbor, I believe we must link love of neighbor with a love of creation. They are all linked. War emerges out of our greed for "natural resources" and our lust for land exploitation. Violence and dehumanization are almost always linked to a broken relationship with creation. We assume—falsely—that civilization brings peacefulness.

To rewild our faith requires reacquainting ourselves with creation. And one of the most practical ways to reacquaint ourselves with creation is to change our relationship with food. There are a number of ways of experimenting with one's relationship with food—from fasting to gardening to fishing. The goal here is to enter into an experiment wherein we engage food in a different way, a way that helps us see ourselves as a part of creation, rather than as beings who live above creation.

One simple practice that has helped me deepen my relationship with the rest of creation is the simple act of cooking a meal. To me, cooking a meal is like making a sand mandala. In Hinduism and Buddhism, a mandala is a geometric pattern that represents the universe. Buddhist monks have a practice where they create beautiful mandalas out of colored sand. When the mandala is finished, they sweep it clean and start anew. The practice of making sand mandalas is an exercise in impermanence. Like life, it is fleeting and dynamic.

Likewise, making a wonderful meal for friends, family, or strangers is an exercise in impermanence. Days before, the food that has now found its way onto a plate was still in the soil (ideally, in soil nearby). It wass grown in a garden or in a field and was picked and prepared with love into a complex collection of flavors, colors, textures, and smells. Every plate is a work of art that still contains life that we consume so that we may live.

When I cook, I don't think about what happened earlier in the day. Nor do I worry about what will happen later in the day. I think about the food. To me, cooking should be done attentively, focusing simply on the act of creating the meal itself.

And when it is ready, I bring it to friends, who are waiting at the table. Some of those friends might have grown the food. Or they rescued it from a dumpster. Or maybe one of them bought it at a local market. The whole process—from the soil to the kitchen, from the plate to the stomach—is itself the art form. And, in its impermanence, is a form of worship.

It is a form of worship that some of us practice several times a day. It is so mundane we may take it for granted. But when we do it attentively and reflect upon the story of the food, we find ourselves participating in creation. A simple meal. What one person sees as a distraction that keeps them from more important things another person may call "Eucharist." And Eucharist is one of those practices that holds the potential to heal rifts that exist between me and someone whom I have hurt, between me and my God, and between me and creation.

Eucharist can be practiced as a sort of ritual with a bit of wine and bread. However, every meal can be eucharistic. How we gather around the table can help heal our relationship with the land when the food we eat is sustainable and honors the fragility of the earth. The time around the table can heal my relationships with the people in my life if the table becomes a place of acceptance, equality, and attention that I carry with me beyond dinner. And the table can serve to bring healing to my relationship with God if I listen to the voice of the Spirit in the voices of those gathered and remember that my brother Jesus once ate a meal with his friends before his crucifixion.

Practice Three: Silence

Most of our lives are loud. It seems to me that most of humanity through-out most of history has experienced ample amounts of silence. Silence was once abundant. Now I find it scarce. Machines hum, music blares, people shout. Rarely do I experience silence. Though, to be honest, rarely do I wel-come it. Silence can be violent—forcing me to sit with myself and my own screaming thoughts. But silence has become a way for me to let go of the false images of God in my head. In silence, where I am free from distrac-tion, I pray the prayer of Meister Eckhart: "God, rid me of God." As various anxieties and random notions enter my mind, I gently dismiss them until I am at peace. And then, like Elijah in the cave at Mount Horeb, the voice of God sometimes comes to me in a gentle whisper.

I used to assume that when God spoke, it was to give me instructions or unveil new truths. But I find that whenever I dismiss everything that isn't of God (as Simone Weil suggests), whatever remains is God. And as I rest in God's presence, I try to resist the temptation to expect anything of God. Rather, I sit. As I sit in silence with God, I trust that God is at work within my soul in unseen wild ways.

Of course, these practices are merely a beginning. We are creative beings. I will find new practices that help me let go of the civilized god in my mind. We all have our own journey. If these practices help you, then practice them, but move deeper. The challenge is to keep experimenting. Some practices will become like trusted friends. But there is always room for new friends. May we all remain open to the wild voice of God, a voice that threatens to tear down the walls that keep us safely in our cages.

CHAPTER SIX GROUP GUIDE

 Summary

A dominant way of understanding God is as a "Supreme Hierarch," the being at the top of the pyramid of power. This God is often understood to be a Great Architect who governs everything with a blueprint or as a Great Ruler who governs with decrees. This sort of God is one to whom we owe allegiance and obedience. This sort of God works well with imperialism. But what if we see God in a more uncivilized way? A feral and wild God who upsets civility and calls us into a faith of radical experimentation?

 Discussion Questions

1. What are some ways of understanding God as someone other than the "Supreme Hierarch"?

2. Have you experienced the presence of God in such a way that it upset or challenged your assumptions or beliefs?

3. The prophets often met God in the wild places, rather than in sacred buildings fashioned by human hands (unlike the priests). What would it look like if our communities related to God as the prophets did more than as the priestly class did?

✘ Group Practice: Nature Meditation

- Walk among the fragments of nature in your surroundings: the trees and flowers and grass in a nearby park or lawn, the plants struggling to free themselves of their cement prisons, the birds and bugs in the air. Your intention is to listen for God's presence in nature. Set aside twenty minutes for this exercise, after which you will be called back together.

- **Breathe.** Before starting to walk, spend a little time standing still. Allow your awareness to be with your body. Take some deep breaths, inhaling deep into the belly. Put your full attention on the sensation of breathing.

- **Walk.** Walk normally, but be aware of your walking: the weight shifting from foot to foot, the moving in and out of breath, the swaying of your arms. When you find yourself distracted by cars or people or other artificial noises, just bring your awareness back to the rhythms of your own body.

- **Notice.** You can next move on to being aware of, and practicing love and gratitude for, the things around you. While inhaling, say to yourself, "I see that you are there." Exhaling, say to yourself, "I thank you for being there." This can be directed at anything you choose: the grass beneath your feet, the flowers or birds or trees around you.

- **Consider.** Select a natural item—a flower, a blade of grass, a bird, a rock—anything that sticks out to you. Pray deeply as you consider this little reflection of God's presence in the world. What does it teach you about God?

- After twenty minutes join back together as a group. Share any insights or reflections.

🕯 Close with a time of prayer.

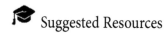 Suggested Resources

Beyond Mere Obedience, by Dorothy Sölle
Original Blessing, by Matthew Fox
Rewilding the Way: Break Free to Follow an Untamed God, by Todd Wynward

A West Bank Liturgy

The sidewalks of this city are my labyrinth
broken bottles and shabby men
roasting coffee and gutter garbage tickle God's nose like the prayers of
the saints
incense of the West Bank
I'm a pilgrim of the streets
looking up from my feet
on the way to Hard Times Cafe

Somali women condemn the cold
businessmen drive through on their daily trek to Temple
gutterpunks on bicycles mock motorists
students still in bed
these icons of the West Bank
I'm a pilgrim of the streets
looking up from my feet
on the way to Hard Times Cafe

Somali men banter on the corner
like crowded pigeons attacking day-old bread
cooing and clucking with tongues of fire
psalms, hymns, and spiritual songs to the God of Abraham
I'm a pilgrim of the streets
looking up from my feet
on the way to Hard Times Cafe

Tree roots crawl through the forgotten soil
challenging, pushing, wriggling free of the confines of their cement overlord
subverting the sidewalk
an arbor day revolution!
a Kyrie for the West Bank
I'm a pilgrim of the streets
looking up from my feet
on the way to Hard Times Cafe

Riverside Plaza rises to the heavens
a Tower of Babel for the Liberal Utopia
its shadow marking the time
across the face of the neighborhood
a silent call to the Divine Office
I'm a pilgrim of the streets
looking up from my feet
on the way to Hard Times Cafe

I'm a pilgrim of the streets
looking up from my feet
on the way to Hard Times Cafe!

7

Walking with the Compassionate Christ

Attention is the rarest and purist form of generosity.

—SIMONE WEIL

JESUS' MINISTRY WAS WONDERFULLY gritty. It wasn't abstract. Jesus made good on his Luke 4 platform by actually proclaiming good news to the poor, setting people free from social exclusion, healing the sick, casting out demons, giving sight to the blind. Sure, there were spiritual implications, but Jesus didn't spiritualize his message. The acts of tangible healing didn't point to a deeper truth. They were, in themselves, a work of liberation and spirituality. He began on the ground, with the people, in a remarkably nonabstract, tangible way.

Yet we start in the opposite way. Often, we spiritualize Jesus and his message and treat the tangible stuff as a sort of heroic option. Some abstract the gospel by spiritualizing it, to the point that the gospel becomes nothing but fodder for books and sermons.

Others abstract the gospel by programming it, to the point where people check the gospel off their list by voting, doing charity work, or simply donating their money to professionals who do the work of the charity on their behalf. Charity, in either case, accepts the unjust arrangement. As Paulo Freire suggests, "The generosity of the oppressors is nourished by an unjust order, which must be maintained in order to justify that generosity ... The man or woman who proclaims devotion to the cause of liberation yet is unable to enter into *communion* with the people, whom he or she continues to regard as totally ignorant, is grievously self-deceived."[1]

Both of these general approaches increase the distance between us and suffering. We become apathetic to the struggles and sufferings around us. Our word *apathy* comes from the Greek word *apatheia*, which is made up of the prefix *a-*, meaning "without," and *pathos*, meaning "suffering." Of the danger of apathy, Dorothee Sölle writes,

> Apathy is a form of the inability to suffer. It is understood as a social condition in which people are so dominated by the goal of avoiding suffering that it becomes a goal to avoid human relationships and contacts altogether. In so far as the experiences of suffering, the *pathai* (Greek for the things that happen to a person, misfortunes) of life are repressed, there is a corresponding disappearance of passion for life and of the strength and intensity of its joys. Without question this ideal bears the imprint of middle-class consciousness.[2]

Jesus rejects apathy. Instead, his is a way of compassion. Compassion comes from the Latin word that means "to suffer with." Compassion rejects apathy and alienation and bridges the distance between persons. Compassion is easily understood, in our society, as a sentiment. Perhaps this is because our society has so thoroughly inherited the separation of action from intention that we feel sentiment is all that is required to be a loving human being. But in Jesus there is no separation between intention and action. His action reflects his heart, just as his life reflects the very life of God.

Rather than a weak sentiment, or a condescending act of charity, compassion is prophetic. Those with compassion refuse to accept the world as it is and enter into injustice and brokenness. Compassion is the practice of mysticism because it collapses the distances between us. And, in bridging the distance, compassion exposes the principalities and powers and myths that breed alienation and separation.

In his classic work *The Prophetic Imagination*, Walter Brueggemann puts it this way:

> Compassion constitutes a radical form of criticism, for it announces that the hurt is to be taken seriously, that the hurt is not to be accepted as normal and natural but is an abnormal and unacceptable condition for humanness . . . Thus the compassion of Jesus is to be understood not simply as a personal emotional reaction but as a public criticism in which he dares to act upon his concern against the entire numbness

1. Freire, *Pedagogy of the Oppressed*, 42–43.
2. Sölle, *Suffering*, 36.

of his social context. Empires live by numbness. Empires, in their militarism, expect numbness about the human cost of war. Corporate economies expect blindness to the cost in terms of poverty and exploitation. Governments and societies of domination go to great lengths to keep the numbness intact. Jesus penetrates the numbness by his compassion and with his compassion takes the first step by making visible the odd abnormality that had become business as usual. Thus compassion that might be seen simply as generous goodwill is in fact criticism of the system, forces, and ideologies that produce the hurt. Jesus enters into the hurt and finally comes to embody it.[3]

The way of Jesus is the way of compassion. It involves sharing life with those around us and suffering with them. I want to be careful here; embracing the suffering of others doesn't require that we treat suffering like a holy fetish. There is a danger in that, particularly for Christians. We worship the One who suffered on a cross. But, as Dorothee Sölle writes, the cross is not "a symbol of masochism which needs suffering in order to convince itself of love. It is above all a symbol of reality. Love does not 'require' the cross, but *de facto* it ends up on the cross. *De facto* Jesus of Nazareth was crucified . . . Love does not cause suffering or produce it, though it must necessarily seek confrontation, since its most important concern is not the avoidance of suffering but the liberation of people."[4]

Jesus went to the cross as an act of solidarity with the oppressed. The cross is God confronting the world with compassion.

As I shared in the introduction, my first mystical experience happened when I was fourteen. As I sat with other teens around a campfire, I experienced the suffering of the world. In the twenty or so years since I've reflected back upon that experience, I've become convinced that it was an invitation to compassion. Throughout my life, I've struggled to accept that invitation.

Every day, when I wake up, I'm aware of my own feelings of alienation. I feel disconnected from people. I feel distant from their pain—even the people I live with—and my own desire to show love and compassion doesn't flow easily. I'm one of those people who loves hugs but is afraid to initiate them.[5]

3. Brueggemann, *Prophetic Imagination*, 88–89.

4. Sölle, *Suffering*, 163–64.

5. I suspect my training to give only "Christian side hugs" may be partly responsible for this.

I tell you this because I don't want you to assume that showing compassion comes easily for me. My own attempts at trying to collapse the distance between me and other human beings have been awkward.

I'll give you a quick example. When folks cry around me (which happens from time to time), I kinda just sit there, looking awkwardly at them. I sometimes ask myself, "What would a compassionate person do in this situation?" My assumption is that when a friend or acquaintance cries, a compassionate person would reach out and hug them or put a hand on their shoulder or something that signifies human connection.

But what I do in such situations is panic inside. I start saying to myself, "Crap, crap, crap, what do I do?" Usually, in the end, what happens is I offer to go make them something to eat. When all else fails, I fall back on what I know.

Yet, as flawed a "wounded healer" as I am, I know I'm more compassionate now than I was last year. And a year ago I was more compassionate than the year before. I am growing in compassion.

One of the temptations I've struggled to overcomes is to equate compassion with charity. I've alluded to this earlier but would like to explore it in further depth here.

Often, First World Christians respond to injustice with charity. Charity never challenges structures of oppression. In fact, charity allows the wealthy and powerful to stay in their position of domination while feeling justified. After all, they are generous with their "earned" wealth. Meanwhile the dispossessed, poor, and marginalized are kept in their place. So much of what begins as a pursuit for justice becomes mere charity in the end.

Charity doesn't, by itself, challenge social relationships. It accepts things as they are and attempts to share a modest portion of the abundance of the "fortunate" with the "less fortunate" (or of the "blessed" with the "needy"). What happens when our institutions bring charity and imperial attitudes into the margins? The history of Christianity shows that the recipients of our "help" become imperial converts who internalize oppression—often assuming that their poverty is their own fault and that, if they are going to be liberated, they need to become like those who give them charity.

We can, unintentionally, make imperial converts.

If we attempt to bring about social justice and relational transformation without first taking a posture of *Gelassenheit*, we will presumptuously carry our imperialism with us into the margins. When Empire enters the margins, it is called "colonization." If we are going to be agents of God's love, then we have to yield our hearts to God for decolonization. This is, painfully, a lifelong process. I don't assume that I'll ever be free from subtly colonizing habits and attitudes. And I certainly won't ever entirely escape from the social privileges afforded to me by virtue of my status as an educated white American male. Nevertheless, out of love for God and neighbor, I need to name these habits, attitudes, and privileges and submit them to God.

Before we can see the kingdom reality, we must first repent of the old order. Before we can experience the joy of the unKingdom, we must mourn over our complicity with Empire. The way of the true radical—the way of the prophet—is to open our eyes to the alternative reality that is the un-Kingdom and to grieve and mourn the world to which we still cling. Sure, there is still room for anger. But above that rises repentance and lament.

We must mourn the old world, the old ways, and its cycle of death—the cycle of greed and violence and oppression—as we move into the unKingdom of God. And, as we do that, we must let go of the illusion of our own righteousness. We can't render ourselves radicals because we happen to have superficially opted out of the system and picked up a new vocabulary.

If we are able to live the part of the radical without mourning our own complicity and mourning for those trapped in the cycle, we are simply a clanging cymbal. If, by some strong exercise of willpower, and through the heat of our frustration, we manage to carve out an entire way of life that stands in contrast to the empire, but we have not love, then we are simply the beat of an angry drum.

Too much justice work has the goal of turning marginalized folks into middle-class Americans. This approach fails to recognize the economic injustices at the root of our economy. Poverty exists because our economic system requires winners and losers. The pursuit of affluence creates poverty.

Our affluence is a deeper problem than their poverty. We need to challenge the logic of capitalism by moving from charity to solidarity.

Within contemporary Christianity many folks believe themselves to be in "solidarity" with all sorts of oppressed people, but somehow they haven't really changed their way of life or the nature of their social lives. We can't challenge injustice by donating money or reading a book. We can't combat racism simply by going to a conference. We don't confront sexism by simply changing the pronouns in our writing and speaking. All of these things are perhaps essential steps in the journey. But they aren't the destination. More needs to change than sentiment. We need to move from charity to compassion. Charity is the sharing of resources. Compassion is the sharing of life and the suffering we experience in life.

PRACTICES FOR WALKING WITH THE COMPASSIONATE CHRIST

So how can we deepen our capacity for compassion? Do we simply muster up the will to do good deeds? Do we read inspirational tales of the saints? Again, I am not going to tell you to do things like practice hospitality or start a soup kitchen. Those may be compassionate acts, but they may also be condescending. Rather, I offer the following practices as things that have helped me deepen in compassion for those around me.

Practice 1: Localizing Our Imaginations

We need to tell the stories of the places in which we live from the vantage point of the oppressed. If we are going to develop practices that show love to one another and the land under our feet, we need to embrace the confessional practice of truth-telling. When I remember that my city, Minneapolis, was born as a staging area to force the Dakota out of land that was deemed more suitable for white settlers, the imperial myths that stifle my imagination lose some of their power over me.

Furthermore, we need to honestly tell the story of how we relate to the places in which we live. If I am going to come to terms with the domination in my own heart, I need to explore my identity in relationship to the place in which I live. This is the only way I can begin to break the "spell" over my imagination that sees myself as an American citizen, or as an individual consumer, or as a thing called a "white man."

One way I practice this happens whenever I take my son to Minnehaha Park in South Minneapolis. Minnehaha Park is near Fort Snelling. Though it is a sacred place to the Dakota, the only monuments there celebrate the European settling of this land. When I take Jonas there, I call it "Oppressor Park" and tell him the story of how white people came to this land. I tell him that the state of Minnesota took the land from the Dakota to make space for white settlers. I also tell him where our family came from (various places in western Europe) and that, while our family didn't take the land, we too are settlers.

I tell him this and then ask him what he thinks about it. Usually, Jonas says something like "Minnesota should give Oppressor Park back to the

Dakota people." I want him to grow up understanding that he is a settler so that he too can see through the allure of imperial myths and instead embrace the unKingdom. In a very important way, telling my little boy such things is my own act of repentance. We tend to tell children (consciously or not) what we hold most true and valuable. By telling him the story of the land, I give myself the freedom to choose a different way. Either I can be a happy imperial citizen or I can work through the layers of conditioning and myth and propaganda and begin, slowly, to relate to the world in truth.

Practice 2: Paying Attention to What Is Happening in Front of Us

Speaking of brainwashing my son, I try to take him to protests from time to time. Jonas committed his first act of civil disobedience when he was a little over a year old. He and I were both guilty of trespassing, but a passerby would have seen a father and son playing in the backyard of a typical South Minneapolis home. As Jonas and I played in the yard with some friends from our faith community, a handful of activists and concerned neighbors were gathered inside, lending their support to Rosemary Williams, a woman who had owned the property for more than twenty years and lived on the block for fifty-five years. Like millions of other USAmericans, Rosemary was facing foreclosure. We were there to hold off the coming eviction, which happened several months later.

Over the past few years, I've taken my son to a handful of protests. He's witnessed an FBI raid, stood with me in solidarity with exploited workers and undocumented friends, and challenged war. I don't assume our attendance at protests does the world any good—at least not directly. I don't protest to effect change in the world. I protest to effect change in me and to show my son a different image of the world.

On September 24th, FBI agents raided six homes in Minneapolis (and two in Chicago) looking for links to "terrorist activity." The eight people targeted by the FBI were respected peace activists who were deemed suspicious because of their travel to Colombia and the Palestinian territories (though travel to both places is legal). But because they were prolific protesters against US military involvement who had traveled to politically sensitive areas, they were flagged.

Jonas was almost three when we went to one of the raids. That sounds scarier than it is. I loaded him into his bicycle trailer and rode up to Hard Times Cafe off Riverside Avenue in Minneapolis. The raid was happening at the apartment above the cafe. The agents were dressed casually as they came out of the apartment door with boxes of confiscated documents and hard drives. Meanwhile, the subject of the raid—a local union organizer and peace activist—was downstairs sitting in the cafe, talking to a local reporter.

I told Jonas what was happening as best as I could. That these guys called the FBI were taking the stuff of a man who only wanted people to stop hurting each other.

When we entered the cafe, I walked over to the activist. Jonas had a concerned look on his face. He said to the man, "I'm sad that those mean FBI guys took your things!" He responded naturally, with compassion. He saw someone experiencing injustice and extended concern.

The next day, we went to a protest outside of the FBI building. A number of peace activists had been raided that day, and the peace community was upset. I wanted Jonas to be ready for the protest, so I went to the local thrift store and bought him a proper uniform—a black turtleneck with an army green blazer. I thought outfitting him like a beatnik would help him look the part of a protester.

The presence of a little beatnik protester at the rally added a human factor, I think. Jonas slowly picked up the chants of the protesters. He heard them chanting "Stand up, fight back!" He too began the chant. When things quieted down for someone to speak, he screamed, "Stand up, fight back!" as loudly as he could. A few dozen people began to chuckle, including the two agents standing at the front door, observing the situation.

This is, of course, not a daily occurrence. Usually, walking in compassion with others involves sitting with guests in our home, or acquaintances we meet on the street. Wherever humanity is, there is an opportunity for compassion. Compassion begins with paying attention. Simone Weil once said that attention is the rarest and purest form of generosity.

It is easy to be overwhelmed by news reports of violent crime and wars and drought and poverty. In fact, it is almost impossible to be anything but apathetic about such things, since they are so abstract and huge. This is why when I read a news report about hundreds dying in a natural disaster or of more than one hundred thousand civilian deaths in Iraq, it doesn't hit me nearly as hard as hearing about a little four-year-old girl getting shot in my city or receiving the news that my grandmother has passed away. Logic doesn't dictate our response to suffering; our proximity to suffering dictates our response to suffering. If we want to challenge the injustices of the world, we need to pay attention to them as they happen around us and respond to them.

Practice 3: Learning in the Margins

Humans are not able to find true compassion, nor can they create structures of deep transformation, without entering into Jesus' own compassion, which is incarnate in the poor and marginalized. Being "aware" of social injustice doesn't collapse the alienation experienced between human beings. We must nurture real relationships, relatively free from agenda, before we develop strong conclusions around what justice looks like.

There is a temptation to enter the margins with the assumption that the folks there are more "needy" than you. Or that they are "less fortunate." Yet Jesus said, "Blessed are the poor." One could fathom the depth of that insight for a lifetime. At the very least, however, it might suggest that the affluent have more to learn at the feet of the poor than they have to teach. I'd like to suggest that we strike such condescending language regarding the poor, the marginalized, or the ostracized. Rather, in a non-sentimentalizing way, let us see our fellow human beings with open eyes, see the world they inhabit for what it is, and see the world with them.

As we break bread in the margins, and the alienation narrows, we may begin to suffer with our new friends. Not a heroic suffering—when we suffer with the oppressed, it isn't a heroic suffering on behalf of another. Rather, we are experiencing a suffering that is ours as well, one that our apathy and privilege has walled away from us.

Lila Watson wrote, "If you have come here to help me, then you are wasting your time . . . But if you have come because your liberation is bound up with mine, then let us work together." By embracing a life of compassion—by suffering with others—we discover our own deep humanity and can begin to live life without abstraction. It is with the marginalized that we can experience the unKingdom of God.

Compassion is costly, but without it, suffering remains. We cannot ignore suffering if we want to see its end. We cannot turn our back on oppression and injustice, nor can we legislate it away. The way of Jesus calls us to compassion. And compassion is something we experience as we learn from Christ in the margins, for that is where Christ dwells. In the words of sixteenth-century Anabaptist martyr Anna of Rotterdam, "Where you hear of the Cross, there is Christ."

Let us go to the places of suffering and learn the way of Jesus.

CHAPTER SEVEN GROUP GUIDE

Summary

Jesus rejects apathy (the way of numbness) and embraces compassion (the way of suffering with others). Compassion isn't warm feelings of goodwill but a move of solidarity where we join with the sufferings of others—sometimes in ways that are very costly. Following Jesus means entering into relationships that confront the injustices and alienating forces of our society so that we can share life with those who suffer.

Discussion Questions

1. In this chapter, the author quotes Dorothee Sölle, who suggests that apathy is "a social condition in which people are so dominated by the goal of avoiding suffering that it becomes a goal to avoid human relationships and contacts altogether . . . This ideal bears the imprint of middle-class consciousness." Does this fit with your experience?

2. What are some of the things you experience that numb you or bring distance between yourself and the struggles of others?

3. In this chapter, the author quotes Walter Brueggeman, who writes, "Governments and societies of domination go to great lengths to keep numbness intact." Why do you think this is?

4. Simone Weil once said, "Attention is the rarest and purest form of generosity." What could it look like for you to give more attention to those in our society that we are conditioned to ignore?

Group Practice: The Cairn of Mourning

- If we want to draw close to the sufferings of others, we must allow ourselves to feel. And as long as we guard our numbness and hold on to our false comforts, we will be unable to give our attention to others.

- In that spirit, you are encouraged to engage in a ritual adapted from the book *Coming Back to Life*, by Joanna Macy and Molly Brown.[6]

---

6. Macy and Brown, Coming Back to Life, 118.

- Participants are invited to bring an object that symbolizes something they are losing, have lost, or are going to lose as they take the way of Jesus seriously. If anyone forgets to bring an object, provide them with paper and pen and allow time for them to draw or write something that expresses their sense of loss. The idea here is to recognize the pain in turning from the old world as we embark more deeply into the new. It is okay to mourn the loss of wealth or prestige or relationships that results when we decide to embrace the compassionate life of Christ.

- Sit in a circle. One by one, at random, people rise and walk to the center and place their object in the center. As they do so, they are to speak of their loss and say, formally, "goodbye." After they have done so, they are to sit back down. Everyone else in the circle is to bear witness by saying, "We hear you."

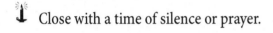 Close with a time of silence or prayer.

 Suggested Resources

Becoming Human, by Jean Vanier
Coming Back to Life, by Joanna Macy and Molly Brown
Suffering, by Dorothy Sölle
Of Gods and Men (film)

The Wind Blows Angry

The wind blows angry
In the lonely places
Where it is free to rage.
Far from the city.

I hear her wailing.
And tremble.
For I wear her wrath,
A threadbare cloak.

The evangelists say, the Breath of God
Is like a gentle Dove.
But to me, she's a raven, consuming the dead.
Or a kestrel, seizing little living things in her talons
And eating them whole.

For the wind blows angry.
Keening in the night.
Giving voice to all who lament.
Whose hopes huddle in shadows.
These alone she comforts.

For the wind blows angry.

8

Discerning the Subversive Spirit

> They paint the Holy Spirit descending upon the Apostles' heads
> in the form of a dove. For shame! Haven't they ever felt the Holy
> Spirit burning them? Where did they find that innocent, edible
> bird? How can they present that to us as Spirit? No, the Holy Spirit
> is not a dove, it is a fire, a man-eating fire which clamps its talons
> into the very crown of saints, martyrs, and great strugglers, reduc-
> ing them to ashes. Abject souls are the ones who take the Holy
> Spirit for a dove which they imagine they can kill and eat.[1]

IN THE BEGINNING, WE find the Spirit hovering over the unformed deep.
There at the beginning, as God spoke light into being, the first spark of
creation.

We know what happens later in Genesis: innocence lost, murder, the
deepening of human frailty and wickedness.

Amidst the shattered fragments of our frail world, the Spirit does her
work—the work of sacred re-creation. It is the Spirit who opens up new
possibilities, new opportunities for God's people to be restored and transformed. Where things fall apart, and the world falls deeper into oppression,
the Spirit subverts.

Subvert is one of my favorite words. It is the combination of two
Latin words: sub, meaning "under," and vertere, meaning "to turn." Subvert

---

1. Kazantzakis, Report to Greco, 508.

means to turn under, to turn upside down, to overturn, to overthrow. A good picture of subversion is what a plow does to soil: it turns it over, letting the good soil emerge from beneath the surface into the sunlight.

The Spirit brings new possibilities to light. The Spirit disrupts the status quo. She refuses to take the world as it is and, instead, flips it. She speaks into our reality, giving us eyes to see things as they are, so that we can deconstruct the world around us and embrace new realities.

The Spirit refuses to accept things as they are and instead woos us down the dangerous path of restoration, re-creation, renovation. We see this throughout the Hebrew Scriptures. Every time God brings about change, the Spirit is present to open eyes, inspire wisdom, reveal forgotten or new truths. It is by the power and influence of the Spirit that we have the great artisans shaping great works (Exod 31:2–5). It is with the voice of the Spirit that the prophets call God's people to faithfulness (Ezek 11). And we are told that it is through the power of this Spirit that things will be made right—justice will come to the nations (Isa 42).

Without the Spirit, we cannot encounter God. It is this Spirit who opens our eyes to see the world-as-it-might-be. It is this Spirit who opens our eyes to see the God-who-is-coming. It is this Spirit who then empowers us to over-turn the world as it is. The Spirit subverts.

When we first encounter the Spirit in the gospels, we see her preparing the way for the Messiah. It is the Spirit who impregnates Mary, it is the Spirit who empowers John to be the greatest prophet, and it is the Spirit who anoints Jesus at his baptism.

The Spirit brings forth the Christ. And then leads him into the desert to be confronted by Satan. From there, we see that Jesus' understanding of his own ministry is tied up with the Spirit, for it is the Spirit's anointing that empowers Jesus to preach good news to the poor.

And it is the Spirit who, after Jesus ascends to the Father, is unleashed upon the disciples—a terrifying wind that leaves flames dancing upon their heads. By the Spirit's power, these disciples start to vomit strange words—a terrifying sign of new unity. A great reversal of Babel, where God fragmented human speech into many languages so that people would scatter. At Pentecost, the fragmented are brought back together.

In Luke 4, Jesus proclaims his Spirit-filled manifesto. Luke and Acts are companion volumes. They are to be read together. In volume one, Jesus is filled with the Spirit at his baptism on the edge of society and then marches to Jerusalem for a final confrontation. In volume two, the followers of Jesus are baptized with the Holy Spirit in Jerusalem and then driven to the edges of the world. The first baptism, that of Jesus, inaugurates the Jubilee. The second baptism, at Pentecost, fulfills it.

In Acts 2, we see the disciples sharing all good things, breaking bread, praying, and listening to apostolic teaching. They too, as the Spirit compels, proclaim good news to the poor, set people free from social exclusion, heal the sick, cast out demons, and give sight to the blind.

It is the Spirit who collapses the distance between people. It is the Spirit who opens our eyes to the reality of God. It is the Spirit who drives us into the wild places. It is the Spirit who brings the Jubilee.

The Spirit not only creates, she destroys. Gone are the old divisions. At Pentecost, the Spirit destroys national distinctions. And later, as the Spirit woos the Gentiles, she destroys the division between Jews and Gentiles.

And every time we see the disciples perform a miraculous deed or utter a bold word, it is the Spirit who enables them to do so. Every missional step forward in the book of Acts is at the Spirit's urging. There is no mission apart from the Spirit.

The Spirit blows where she will. She is never commanded, never used. She is unpredictable. And mysterious. She is a dangerous bird. She subverts. And when she burns in your heart, she destroys you from within, so that a new life may rise from the ashes.

The Spirit has quietly ripped apart the old world and is bringing forth the new. Within us. Let us listen to the Spirit.

A CRISIS OF IDENTITY

As we let go of our blueprints in the presence of the Feral God and embrace the way of compassion, the temptation is to quickly move forward to draft a new blueprint. At the same time, we are tempted either to distance ourselves from the pain around us or, like so many before us, to allow our hearts to grow numb. When I am in that place—armed with a clever plan and cut off from the depths of humanity around me—it is almost impossible for me to participate with the Spirit. I say "almost" because the Spirit still finds a way to wake me from the slumber of my own power.

Relationships are dynamic, not static. Relationships that become static fall apart. Anyone who has been in a long-term relationship understands this. In this way, we are never done repenting, turning away from those things that bring about distance, abstraction, and alienation. We are never finished in our task to move more deeply into the love of God.

This is a book about repentance. Repenting not only means turning away: letting go of those myths and things that encumber love. It is also about paying attention to the world with eyes of compassion. And then acting.

The previous two chapters explored the postures that help us see the world differently, to see one another differently, to see God differently. I wrote about the wild undoing that is the Feral God. And I wrote about the compassionate way of Jesus. Now I will turn to our role in participating with the subversion of the Spirit. This participation requires discernment. It would be unwise to leap into the world, seeking to change it, without discerning our way forward.

Our inability to discern has fostered an identity crisis in the church. The church does not know what it is. It is pulled between the way of Empire and the way of Jesus. That crisis has come from a failure to discern. Our vision has been co-opted. Many of us are so enamored with the American Dream that it is nearly impossible to see the unKingdom of God. Nevertheless, we continue enacting bold plans. We invest billions in ministry schemes. We go around the world, sowing the seeds of faith. All the while, we assume that we are doing the work of the Spirit. Yet rarely do we stop to listen, to discern together the way the Spirit would have us act.

At best, failing to discern the leading of the Spirit results in a massive waste of resources as we forge ahead with our Spiritless agendas. At worst, it has disastrous results for those experiencing oppression. How many have experienced pain as a result of the well-intentioned actions of the presumed faithful?

Christians in the so-called First World are continually presented with the temptation to, upon acquiring radical insights, go out and "try to change the world." They assume the strength of those insights will leave a deeper footprint than the hidden, unquestioned assumptions that bear the weight of Christian imperialism.

We go into the world, relying upon the fruits of imperialism—formal education, wealth, entrepreneurial skills—to "bring the Kingdom."

SUBVERTING MISSIO DEI

In 2003, my wife and I set out to form an urban church called Missio Dei. I was a seminary student with bold and radical ideas. Or so I thought. We went through training, raised a bunch of money, and launched a hip urban worship service. In that first year, I raised and spent roughly $50,000.

A year into it, things were going okay. We had as many attendees as could generally be expected for a new urban church—about forty or so people. But few, if any, actually lived in the city; they commuted in from the suburbs. And all of the money was basically going to pay my salary and cover the rent for a once-a-week worship space. I felt like a fraud. This wasn't the way of Jesus.

So I did what anyone probably should do in my situation. I quit. I said I was done being a pastor. I sat down with everyone who considered Missio Dei their church and told them, "My job right now as your pastor is to help you find a new church."

It sucked. My wife and I started sliding into the sort of debt one incurs when having school expenses, a mortgage, and no job.

We decided to have a retreat for the few folks who wanted to discern what would come next. We met in a cheap cabin in Wisconsin. My wife and I were joined by a handful of folks who really had nowhere else to go. Several of them just happened to be living at our house at that time; they had received hospitality and just wanted to be a part of what, if anything, would come next.

I immediately started going into planning mode . . . but every time I started going down that road, it felt hollow. I had just lost my dream church because my plans hadn't worked. I knew in my soul that I needed to shut up. Together, we needed to listen.

I wish I could remember what it was that shifted the conversation. But as eight of us gathered in a cabin in rural Wisconsin, something shifted. We decided to center our lives around hospitality, simplicity, and prayer. It didn't seem heroic or even exciting at the time. It just felt faithful. That was in the days before intentional communities were trendy. The following eight years were tremendously difficult—and amazingly clarifying. We began to cultivate the practice of communal discernment.

PRACTICES FOR DISCERNING THE SUBVERSIVE SPIRIT

We still have a long way to go, but I've learned some things about listening to the Spirit together as a community. I'd like to share several of the practices that I've found particularly helpful. Again, this list isn't exhaustive. There are others that may be much more helpful to you and your community. Yet

I offer what I've experienced in the hope that it might serve you. It may also be helpful to dismiss the idea that discernment is a way of receiving marching orders from a Sky General or a blueprint from the Divine Architect. God's will is more like an invitation to life than anything else. And it is ongoing. It isn't a mechanistic process of discovering God's will and then executing that will.

Practice 1: Open Worship

I'm immensely indebted to the Quaker tradition for teaching me about discernment. I'm also indebted to the work of John Howard Yoder. His book *Body Politics* is an amazing primer for church practices. Of the various practices Yoder describes, I'd like to focus on one he calls "the Rule of Paul" (and most Quakers call "open worship"). Drawing from 1 Corinthians 14, the Rule of Paul invites those gathered to speak as led by the Holy Spirit. When finished, the speaker is to yield the floor to the next speaker. Yoder suggests that "consensus arises uncoerced out of open conversation. There is no voting in which a majority overuns a minority and no decision of a leader by virtue of his office."[2]

The Rule of Paul is, basically, that everyone is given the floor as they feel led by the Holy Spirit. And any decisions are to be made by consensus. This is considered impractical by many—particularly when it comes to important decisions. As difficult as it can sometimes be, our community has practiced open worship in one form or another for eight years and we've never had a decision-making crisis.

At the Mennonite Worker we practice the Rule of Paul in two different contexts. Often, we meet on Saturday mornings to discern through issues facing our community. In this meeting we encourage folks to speak even if they aren't sure they are being led by the Spirit. We want everyone's voice to be heard if it is a matter that they care about. There is a good deal of discussion. A facilitator is designated to make sure everyone gets a chance to speak. The facilitator also calls us to times of silence or prayer when we're "stuck."

We also set aside at least twenty minutes during our Sunday evening worship gathering to listen together in silence. In this meeting, folks are encouraged to speak (or sing) if the Spirit stirs. Decision-making need not be the goal. We want to listen to the Holy Spirit, rather than simply reading about how the Holy Spirit communicated to dead apostles. In a noisy world

2. Yoder, *Body Politics*, 67.

of over-information, communal discernment is more essential than ever. Taking time to sit in silence together as we calm our thoughts and allow the Spirit to move in us is important. It is important even if nothing is said. For even the silence communicates the possibility of God moving us beyond our best plans as we wait together for a new world.

Practice 2: Naming and Resisting

One of the five core values of the Mennonite Worker is resistance (the others are hospitality, simplicity, prayer, and peacemaking). Often, folks ask me, "Why do you include resistance? Isn't it enough to be *for* something? Why do you need to be *against* something?" Repentance requires both a turning *from* and a turning *toward*. We are called to struggle against the principalities and powers as we seek to walk in the way of Jesus. Like the story of the Zen master (which I told in chapter 3), how are we going to learn the way of Jesus if we don't empty our cups first? This emptying begins with naming the principalities and powers around us—by naming the myths that we've discovered. And, from there, we discern a tangible way of resisting.

I've found the following questions to be an important way of naming and resisting the principalities and powers:

1. What is a great evil or injustice we (or our friends) are experiencing in society?

2. What lies or myths do people believe that keep this injustice from being challenged?

3. What is the clearest expression of that evil or injustice? The goal isn't to name the worst expression, but the clearest.

4. How do we currently relate to that injustice or evil? How do we relate to that expression?

After deeply exploring these questions, we can move to the next questions in a posture of discernment.

5. Is there anything we can do to confront that expression?

6. Is there anything we can do to expose those myths or lies?

For example, Dr. King might have suggested that racism is the greatest injustice he and his friends were experiencing in society. One of the powerful myths in the civil rights era was the myth of "separate but equal." Racism took (and takes) many forms. But the clearest expressions of racism in the civil rights era was segregation, which was demonstrated with separate drinking fountains, separate schools, whites-only establishments, whites-only seating areas on public buses, etc. Organizers confronted that segregation with tactics like the Montgomery bus boycott or lunch counter sit-ins.

Of course, the example I'm giving involves a marginalized group (African Americans) resisting oppression. Things get trickier when those of the dominant group or class attempt to confront injustice. There is a danger of doing resistance without being attentive to our own complicity with the very thing we're trying to resist. It is important, particularly with justice work, to examine our own identities and cultivate a practice of compassion before we jump in to address societal injustice.

Practice 3: Arguing with Jesus

This may seem like a strange suggestion, but it has changed my relationship with Jesus. In most relationships, a lack of honesty creates a barrier to vulnerability. This seems obvious. Nevertheless, I've met so many people who are unwilling to be honest with their struggles with Jesus. One of the things we did when our community "started over" was to ask a few questions whenever we read from the gospels:

1. What is Jesus saying or doing in this passage?
2. What is it within us that rises up in opposition to this? What don't I like about this? What confuses me?
3. Is it possible that this tension is inviting us to reconsider the passage?
4. Is it possible that this tension is inviting me to let go of something?

After exploring these questions, we'd follow up with this one:

5. What would it look like for us to do likewise?

The last question is dangerous. There is a temptation to "blueprint" here. In fact, it was our struggle to discern creative responses that led us to embrace the previous two practices. Nevertheless, if we are going to walk in the way of Jesus, we need to be honest with ourselves. Pretenses must fall. By being honest with the Gospels, in particular, and the Scriptures in general, we give space for the Holy Spirit to move among us. The goal here is not simply to conform to what Scripture says. We must yield our hearts to the Spirit until we are able to move forward. The Spirit desires our participation in re-creation, not our mere obedience.

These practices aren't complete. I share them together because I believe that open worship, or something like it, is an excellent context for group spiritual discernment. And in that context, we can grapple with the positive vision of Jesus while also grappling with the influences of the principalities and powers.

As we honestly encounter the way of Jesus and honestly engage the injustices in our society, we can begin to discern a way forward together. My hope and prayer for those reading this book is that this discernment is rooted in compassion and in the wild freedom of a God who calls us to embrace the fullness of life.

CHAPTER EIGHT GROUP GUIDE

 Summary

Wherever the Spirit is at work, a new world is possible. The Holy Spirit is subversive—confronting the old world and birthing a new world. If we are going to participate in this new world, we must discern the presence of the Spirit.

 Discuss the questions in the section titled "Practices for Discerning the Subversive Spirit":

1. What is a great evil or injustice we (or our friends) are experiencing in society?

2. What lies or myths do people believe that keep this injustice from being challenged?

3. What is the clearest expression of that evil or injustice? The goal isn't to name the *worst* expression, but the *clearest*.

4. How do we currently relate to that injustice or evil? How do we relate to that expression?

After deeply exploring these questions, move to the next two questions in a posture of discernment.

5. Is there anything we can do to confront that expression?

6. Is there anything we can do to expose those myths or lies?

 Group Practice

Commit as a group to a simple next step based on your answer to #5 or #6 above. The best responses confront and expose in the same act.

 Close with a time of silence or prayer.

 Suggested Resources

The Call to Discernment in Troubled Times, by Dean Brackley
The Soul of Discernment, by Elizabeth Liebert
Discernment: Reading the Signs of Daily Life, by Henri Nouwen

Jesus Lives

Jesus lives
in the spicy smell
of the bundled man
on the bus station floor.
Jesus lives
on those three blank pages
at the front
of the preacher's Bible.
Jesus lives
in the day-old bread
used to make French toast
you'll eat alone.
Jesus lives
in the wine box
never opened
at the suburban dinner party.
We live
when we give our attention
to the forgotten.

9

Gathering around the
Revolutionary Table

Love casts out fear, but we have to get over the fear in order to get
close enough to love them.

—Dorothy Day

Before we can create a new world together, we must believe a new
world is possible. Most people in our society, I suspect, don't believe an
alternative is possible. Nor do they really want a different world.

We are unable to imagine a society where there are no poor or where
there are no rich. Even if we could imagine such a society, would we really
be interested in living in it?

We are all subject to what psychologist Bruce Levine calls
"zombification"[1]—where we are largely hypnotized by television, by adver-
tising, by bureaucracy. We have a diminished capacity to get upset. We are
lulled into a sense of false comfort.

As long as we can get enough to eat (no matter where the food comes
from), can watch our favorite shows, can log into our Facebook, and have a
roof over our heads, most of us are content—at least content enough to stay

---

1. Levine, *Get Up, Stand Up*, 63.

invested in the way things are, more or less. We may want change, but only to a degree. We want tweaks, not revolution.

Part of the anesthesia of our society is consumer culture. Of the many things that our society excels at, few rival our penchant for buying and selling. We are constantly bombarded with an ever-increasing array of stuff. And we are conditioned by it. Shopping is a sacrament. We have been raised with an intense awareness that we lack and that the only remedy is money. Our lives are spent trying to buy ourselves whole.

This wayward attempt to satisfy our culturally conditioned greed has resulted in environmental degradation, oil wars, and social noise. But it has also resulted in spiritual vapidity.

Meanwhile, we are fragmented. We are bombarded with ethical decisions and consumer choices. We are stressed and lonely and tired. We find ourselves with an overdeveloped sense of lack. We are encouraged to shop or surf our way to wholeness. Even spirituality, which should be our way out of this trap, has largely been repackaged and digitized for easy consumption.

But it doesn't have to be this way.

THOSE HOLY HIPPIES

The early church was like a hippy commune, but with fewer orgies (I'm guessing).

According to the book of Acts, "All the believers were one in heart and mind. No one claimed that any of their possessions was their own, but they shared everything they had . . . And God's grace was so powerfully at work in them all that there were no needy persons among them" (4:32–34).

Sounds nice, doesn't it? Can you imagine being part of a group of one heart and mind, where you love each other so much that you meet all of one another's needs?

Isn't that what we spend our whole lives trying to achieve? We work hard to have enough money to take care of all of our needs but try not to work so hard that we can't share our life with those we love.

How is that working for you?

Sometimes you'll find a family that experiences something like this, but can you imagine an entire movement of people—many who were once strangers—from diverse social and economic backgrounds living like this?

Neither can I. But it was Jesus' vision for his movement. And it meant that everyone had to share.

Let's unpack Jesus' vision a bit more:

> A certain ruler asked him, "Good teacher, what must I do to inherit eternal life?"
>
> "Why do you call me good?" Jesus answered. "No one is good—except God alone. You know the commandments: 'You shall not commit adultery, you shall not murder, you shall not steal, you shall not give false testimony, honor your father and mother.'"
>
> "All these I have kept since I was a boy," he said.
>
> When Jesus heard this, he said to him, "You still lack one thing. Sell everything you have and give to the poor, and you will have treasure in heaven. Then come, follow me."
>
> When he heard this, he became very sad, because he was very wealthy. Jesus looked at him and said, "How hard it is for the rich to enter the kingdom of God! Indeed, it is easier for a camel to go through the eye of a needle than for the rich to enter the kingdom of God." (Luke 18:18–25)

If I had a "top five most dismissed passages of the New Testament" list, this passage would make it. In fact, I have yet to meet a wealthy person who feels it applies to them.

Most folks dismiss this passage by suggesting that Jesus knew the heart of the "rich young ruler" and knew that he had a personal problem with wealth, which, thankfully, isn't really such a problem among twenty-first-century American Christians. This logic assumes that the rich man's wealth is incidental—Luke could've just as easily written about the angry young ruler, the promiscuous young ruler, or perhaps the cussing young ruler. In the case of the latter, the young cusser would have become very sad because he was prone to saying the word *shit*. Jesus would then have looked at him and said, "How hard is it for the potty-mouthed to enter the kingdom of God!"

Unfortunately, this doesn't work. The Gospel of Luke talks about wealth and poverty—a lot. Jesus tells not only the rich young ruler to sell everything but also his disciples. In Luke 12, Jesus tells his followers, "Do not be afraid, little flock, for your Father has been pleased to give you the kingdom. Sell your possessions and give to the poor. Provide purses for yourselves that will not wear out, a treasure in heaven that will never fail, where no thief comes near and no moth destroys" (vv. 32–33). Jesus' concerns about wealth extended much further than one rich young ruler.

In fact, in Jesus' inaugural address—the first sermon he gives in his public ministry—he essentially proclaims that the Jubilee has come:

> "The Spirit of the Lord is on me,
> because he has anointed me
> to proclaim good news to the poor.
> He has sent me to proclaim freedom for the prisoners
> and recovery of sight for the blind,
> to set the oppressed free,
> to proclaim the year of the Lord's favor."
> Then he rolled up the scroll, gave it back to the attendant and sat down.
> The eyes of everyone in the synagogue were fastened on him. He began
> by saying to them, "Today this scripture is fulfilled in your hearing."
> (Luke 4:18–21)

Many scholars agree that "the year of the Lord's favor"—which is found originally in Isaiah 61—refers to the institution of the Jubilee.

According to the Hebrew Jubilee (which, at the very least, informed Jesus' approach to economics), if someone has amassed wealth, it doesn't *necessarily* matter if it comes directly at the expense of the poor. Hoarding was stealing from the poor, *intrinsically*. And, as such, it would have been unjust. Look at Leviticus 25 to read more on what God was going for with the Jubilee—it meant canceling all debts, returning land to the previous occupants, and ending all slavery. It was liberation. It was a great big sociopolitical ctrl-alt-delete. It was a rebooting of the system—an end to injustice.

But Jesus wasn't asking Israel to start practicing Jubilee every fifty years. Instead, as biblical scholar N. T. Wright suggests, in this passage Jesus used Jubilee language to point to what he envisioned as an *ongoing practice*—rather than being undertaken once every fifty years by Israel, Jubilee was to be practiced every day by the disciples.[2]

An honest reading of Luke-Acts makes this clear. The early church lived in a way that we today would see as communistic. Nevertheless, whenever I talk to folks about Jesus' call to Jubilee, people push back—especially if they have money.

The modern USAmerican understanding of justice is quite different than the justice of Jesus. Nowhere can we find in his Jubilee vision that a

---

2. Wright, *Jesus and the Victory of God*, 294–95.

wealthy person needs only to give alms to be justified, since wealth comes from the land, and the land, which ultimately belongs to God, is granted to the people of God. In light of this, the wealthy aren't called to mere charity. Charity doesn't get at justice. Even when Jubilee ceases to be rooted in the promised land, it is still assumed that, in Christ, everything belongs to the Lord and should, therefore, be redistributed to those in need as an act of justice—not as an act of "charity."

In other words, Jesus never intended for some of his followers to be wealthy while others remained poor.

And, in the beginning, it seems that the church actually practiced Jubilee. In the early chapters of Acts, we see a church where all needs are met. Folks would sell everything they had and share the proceeds to care for one another. They didn't see it as an act of charity—charity accepts the status quo. When we do charity, we give out of our affluence to help the poor; we don't actually sacrifice our affluence to destroy the distinction between the rich and the poor.

No, the early church wasn't charitable. They were revolutionary. They lived, for a short time, in Jubilee.

When we love each other, we share all good things with one another. Love applied to economics is Jubilee. Love means risking one's economic security to share. When Jesus spoke of money, he didn't challenge the wealthy because they were mean to poor people. Rather, he challenged them because they put their own security above the needs of their neighbors.

And so, the challenge issued to the rich young ruler wasn't to start being charitable but to remove the very thing that divided him from his poor sisters and brothers—his wealth. By selling everything he had, he could purchase kinship with the poor and thus be among them in the unKingdom of God. And this is our challenge as well.

In Luke 6:20, Jesus says, "Blessed are you who are poor, for yours is the kingdom." The unKingdom of God is for the poor. And, impossibly, it is for the rich who practice Jubilee by sharing all good things with the poor.

But sharing all good things with the poor isn't a heroic act. We don't earn an extra jewel in our heaven-crowns for it. It is simply the most human thing we can do. It is a simple and honest act of love.

We often use Jesus as an example of downward mobility. It is assumed that, in heaven, Jesus was kinda wealthy—and that he left that all behind to slum it with the poor folks. But Jesus isn't simply someone who decided to serve the poor. He was poor. He didn't speak as an affluent advocate for the poor; he spoke as a representative of the poor. I wonder if Jesus pitied the rich young ruler more than the poor lepers he healed? After all, it was the young man's enmeshment with wealth that kept him from inheriting eternal life.

Whether Jesus addressed the wealthy or the poor, his goal was to call folks into a righteous relationship with God and neighbor. Jesus' sermons and acts serve to convert the marginalized into human beings. His are acts of liberation for the oppressed and the poor.

But what of the rich and the powerful? In this encounter with the rich young ruler, we see the way that they are to enter into the unKingdom. They also need to be converted into human beings.

If the poor become marginalized and dehumanized because of oppressive power and the crushing weight of social, economic, and religious systems, then the ones who wield that power and create or support those systems also become dehumanized, but in a different way.

In fact, if you read through Luke-Acts carefully, it becomes apparent that Luke isn't simply rejecting the wealthy (it is valid to believe that Luke himself was wealthy at some point) but is instead deeply interested in the salvation of the wealthy.

But let's get practical. What is, ultimately, the goal of the wealthy divesting their wealth? The goal is to share possessions . . . which is what we see in the early chapters of Acts. When wealthy people come to faith, they are to share everything with the poor, who receive it. But the poor and the wealthy don't then go their separate ways; rather, they live as family. The goal of downward mobility isn't mere charity but solidarity.

Thus, Jesus opens for us an economic vision that destroys the economic divisions between people. It is a vision that is firmly within our reach. It doesn't require an overhaul of the "system." It simply requires that a group of people live like family across class lines. Simple, right?

OF JULIBEES AND GUMMY BEARS

One night about five years ago, we were finishing a Wednesday community meal. On this particular night, there were probably a dozen people gathered around the table. We were feeling good—we didn't want the night to end.

"Lets go to a movie!" someone suggested.

Within minutes, an outing was planned.

At this point it might be worth mentioning that I have two major weaknesses (well, more than two, but I'm only going to share two with you right now): gummy bears and movies. I will never say no to either. My mind is a sad sponge, having absorbed thousands of meaningless film hours. And my body is a sad sponge as well—having absorbed hundreds of pounds of gummies.

One day, when my wife was out of town visiting her parents, I ate a five-pound bag of gummy bears. And I'd do it again.

On this particular occasion, I'm not sure which movie we saw. I've seen thousands of movies. I don't really remember who went on the outing either. I can only be certain of two things:

1. I ate gummies at the movie.
2. Don wasn't there.

Over the eight years thus far of the Mennonite Worker's existence, we've received dozens of guests. Don (not his real name) stands out as a guest for a number of reasons. He had lost his apartment because he lost his job. He lost his job because he was no longer able to work. He was unable to work because his chemotherapy made him weak. And on top of all of that, he was HIV positive.

Don was one of the warmest, kindest guests we've ever had.

That night Don wasn't at the movie because he didn't have money to go to the movie. I suppose I could have bought him a ticket . . . but that would have meant not getting gummy bears.

I can be an idiot sometimes.

The truth is, in many small and large ways, we do the same thing every day. It usually comes down to a choice between having more for ourselves or sharing what we have with others.

To Jesus, Mammon (which is an interesting Aramaic word that is perhaps best translated as "wealth") is like a false god who woos away the rich and keeps them from being in community with the people of God. And it is a force that enslaves the poor, keeping them from awaking to their full humanity. Mammon isn't a neutral thing—it is a perilous tool that can either purchase solidarity or serve as a wall dividing the wealthy from the poor.

Jesus doesn't say, "Where your heart is, there is your treasure"; he says, "Where your treasure is, there is your heart." The difference is important.

Let me put it this way: Jesus says that our hearts follow after our treasure like a dog runs after a stick. How we spend our money (or our resources) determines where our heart will be—what kind of a person we'll be. There is, at least in Jesus' teachings, no such thing as a hoarder whose heart is with the poor. Solidarity isn't a sentiment.

So, like the rich young ruler, we USAmericans are being asked to use our wealth to embrace Jubilee. We are being invited to participate in the sort of society that looks like a family, where we are of one heart and one mind, and where no one is needy.

BEYOND ECONOMICS

On Saturdays, we used to gather at the empty lot across from Palmer's Bar in Minneapolis to serve vegan chili to the neighborhood. We called this weekly ritual the Hospitality Train—the line of bicycles hauling trailers filled with a propane burner, buckets (to be used as chairs), a canopy, a large pot, serving utensils, etc., reminded us of a train.

One day, I took a break from the Hospitality Train and walked down Cedar Avenue to get a soda from West Bank Grocery—one of the small, Somali-owned groceries in the area. As I walked, I noticed a man on the far end of the block walking toward me. Even at that distance, I sensed he was homeless; he was clothed with too many layers for a warm day and was hauling a large backpack.

As he got closer, I saw that he walked with a heavy limp. He was wearing glasses with one lens blacked out. And he was looking at me with a smile on his face.

It seemed likely that he was going to ask me for money. Usually, when someone approaches me for money, it comes with some sort of story. These stories usually sound the same. There is the classic "I need money for gas because my car broke down a few miles away" or "I need money for the bus to visit my sick wife (or child)." Sometimes the story is more elaborate, offering a rapid-fire account of all the miseries in life that my $2 can help alleviate.

Often in those cases, I'd feel a mixture of sympathy and frustration. I'd feel sympathetic because most people end up on the streets for legitimately sad reasons. Few people end up homeless for happy reasons. But I'd also feel frustration because I didn't like the feeling of doubting someone's story.

I wanted to live in a world where folks told the truth. In the end, I almost always give cash if I have it, because being homeless is hard work.

As this man walked toward me on the sidewalk, I began to feel that helpless combination of sympathy and frustration. I started to wonder what sort of bullshit story he'd tell me and what sort of response I might give that could strike the perfect balance between compassion and frugality.

As my mind pondered these things, I unexpectedly felt God's presence, along with the words "Give him whatever he asks for."

I didn't have time to think things over before the man stopped and asked, "Can I have $5?"

I was stunned. I'm not sure which surprised me more—that God had decided to speak into my mind or that this man had simply asked for a specific amount of money without an accompanying story.

I was so surprised that I responded with untypical candor: "Good thing you didn't ask for $100!"

The smile left his face as it twisted into an expression of confusion.

"As I saw you walking toward me, I felt God tell me to give you whatever you asked for . . . so thank you for just asking for $5," I said, smiling.

Upon hearing my explanation, he took off his backpack and removed a wire bound notebook. With excitement, he shared a couple of his poems, which he had written to Jesus.

That was how I became friends with Michael.

I'd like to tell you that we lived happily ever after. But in the years since that mystical encounter on the street—where God spoke into my experience and tore down, if only for a few minutes, the walls of separation between Michael and me—we have caused each other a great deal of pain.

In the few weeks following that first meeting, I came to learn a bit of Michael's story. I learned of his history of abuse and his time in and out of jail. At the time, Michael was in his mid-fifties. He had spent a significant part of his adulthood on the streets. A lot of that had to do with his addictions, which mostly served as a way of self-medicating psychological and physical pain.

During those first few weeks, he started calling me "big brother." He'd introduce me to strangers that way: "Hey, this is my big brother Mark." This was strange for several reasons. Not only was he twenty years my senior, he was also a good nine inches shorter than me. He was black and I am white.

I began to call him my brother too. I even started ending conversations with "I love you, brother." Now, that may seem like a small thing to you. But for some men (like me) who've been shaped by the sort of emotionally repressive, stoic culture of rural white Minnesota, it was a big deal. To this day, I've probably said "I love you" to fewer than ten people.

Then, one day, Michael asked if he could crash at our house for a few days. This wasn't an unexpected request. At that time, my wife and I were living with a few others from the Mennonite Worker. We had decided to maintain a guest room for folks in need of lodging. I assumed it would be fine. But I told him I needed to check with my housemates first.

There were six people living in our house at that time. Five agreed to extend hospitality to Michael. One refused. And since we had agreed to make these sorts of decisions by consensus, I had to tell Michael that he wasn't welcome in my home.

I was hurt and angry. I felt like a hypocrite—here I was calling a man "brother," and I couldn't even let him sleep on a couch for a few days.

Michael took the rejection relatively well, I thought. "He's homeless, he's probably used to this sort of thing," I thought to myself.

That evening, he hit the bottle hard and was picked up by the police for a "drunk and disorderly" charge. Since it was a violation of his probation, he went to jail for a year.

It was one of the worst nights of my life. I remember screaming and crying into my pillow as my wife feebly tried to console me. I felt like a hypocrite—I said one thing yet did another. My treatment of Michael, as reasonable as it may seem to so many people, felt like a betrayal of the gospel.

A COOTIE INFESTATION

It is easy to exclude people; we do it all the time. Often, we have little reason. Sometimes our exclusion is based upon national borders or ethnic identities. Sometimes it is because of religion. Perhaps they just look strange and make us feel uncomfortable. In the case of Michael, we excluded him because he was a homeless black man. When we exclude someone simply because they are a certain type of person, we are guilty of something called sociomoral disgust. Psychologist Richard Beck writes,

> In sociomoral disgust people and entire populations can be seen as sources of contamination. Thus, contact with these persons can elicit the strong revulsion of the disgust response . . . Sociomoral disgust can extend, on a case-by-case basis, to individuals we deem "disgusting," "revolting," or "creepy." We make these attributions for a variety of reasons, (e.g., poor hygiene, moral failures).

Regardless as to the source of the attribution, we experience feelings of revulsion in proximity to these people . . . Sociomoral disgust can [also] apply to entire populations . . . Wherever hate, racism, or genocidal impulses exist, sociomoral contamination and disgust take center stage.[3]

You'd think that first-century Israel had a cootie infestation. In child-lore, cooties is a sort of imaginative infectious disease—a way of marking those kids who should be excluded for a variety of reasons. What seems relatively "harmless" on a playground becomes absolutely wicked at the sociopolitical level.

The Pharisees maintained a system of social exclusion. Of course, Romans and other Gentiles were off limits. But even fellow Jews labeled "sinners" and "tax collectors" certainly had cooties. These weren't simply people to be avoided for their bad influence; they were labeled "unclean." It was a way of ritualizing and spiritualizing exclusion.

In his book *Unclean*, Dr. Beck makes the case that Jesus' words and actions directly challenged the way in which sociomoral disgust operated in his society. In Matthew 9:9–13 we read,

> As Jesus went on from there, he saw a man named Matthew sitting at the tax collector's booth. "Follow me," he told him, and Matthew got up and followed him.
>
> While Jesus was having dinner at Matthew's house, many tax collectors and sinners came and ate with him and his disciples. When the Pharisees saw this, they asked his disciples, "Why does your teacher eat with tax collectors and sinners?"
>
> On hearing this, Jesus said, "It is not the healthy who need a doctor, but the sick. But go and learn what this means: 'I desire mercy, not sacrifice.' For I have not come to call the righteous, but sinners."

Throughout the gospels, Jesus offends the Pharisees with the company he keeps. To the Pharisees, holiness was maintained by excluding the unclean. Jesus smashed their notions of holiness. It was a big no-no to be a guest in the home of a disreputable person. It still is today, but even more so back then. Few things were more upsetting to the religious establishment of Jesus' day than who he ate with. He ate with tax collectors—who were considered national traitors and religious rejects. He ate with prostitutes. He ate with "sinners" (in those days, calling a person "sinner" was like calling

---

3. Beck, *Unclean*, 74.

them trash). It was much deeper than cootie-violation. Jesus was including folks who were traitors, folks who were immoral. And by sitting at table with them, it was assumed he was contaminated by them.

But Jesus' offense goes much deeper than that. In Matthew 8:1–4, an unclean man, a leper, comes before Jesus, begging to be healed, saying, "Lord, if you are willing, you can make me clean." Jesus reaches out and touches him (thus making himself ceremonially unclean) and only *then* heals him. Jesus was willing to make himself unclean before he cleansed others. We see this throughout the gospels—Jesus associates with sinners before they fully leave their sin behind. He meets them where they are in order to call them. He doesn't stand outside of their lives, calling them out, waiting for them to get their act together before embracing them. We should be grateful for this, otherwise we'd all be left on our own.

Jesus' actions weren't merely compassionate. They were seen as destructive, as a threat to the fabric of his society. He was willing to transgress social boundaries wherever he found them.

Let's go back to Jesus' words in Matthew 9: "It is not the healthy who need a doctor, but the sick. But go and learn what this means: *'I desire mercy, not sacrifice.'* For I have not come to call the righteous, but sinners."

What is Jesus getting at here? This phrase "I desire mercy, not sacrifice" is repeated in Matthew 12 when the Pharisees get upset with Jesus and the disciples for picking grain and healing on the Sabbath.

"Sacrifice" refers to that mechanism for ritual cleansing and repentance. It is the impulse toward purity that marks off and excludes that which is not holy. It maintains the boundary between clean and unclean, holy and unholy. To show mercy, however, is about crossing purity boundaries. To show mercy is to include and embrace the "undeserving"—outsiders, the unclean, the sinner.

According to Dr. Beck, mercy and sacrifice are "intrinsically incompatible." Jesus was forced to choose between the priestly role of maintaining purity or the prophetic role of seeking justice. To Jesus, the Pharisaic pursuit of purity alienated whole groups of people. But their fixation on purity was itself a reaction to earlier generations of religious intermingling and loose morality.

Jesus' way around this impasse wasn't simply to reject the purity impulse. Rather, he reverses it. Beck writes, "Rather than the unclean polluting the clean, we see, in Jesus' touch, the clean making the polluted pure.

Here, in Jesus, we see a reversal, a *positive contamination*. Contact *cleanses* rather than pollutes."[4]

In Jesus' approach, being godly is more about who we include than who we exclude. If our first impulse is holiness, we'll set boundaries to protect ourselves. If our first impulse is mercy, we'll cross boundaries, showing love and hospitality to those who are perhaps hardest for us to love. Using the analogy of the playground, we must start spreading "good cooties" of inclusion, and we must first go to those who have felt most left out.

But few of us play the cooties game anymore. Few of us divide our social worlds into "clean" and "unclean." But we can imagine those in our society that we hold in contempt. We can imagine those people we'd feel uncomfortable sitting next to on a bus.

In my neighborhood, I have seen young, clean-cut white folks cross to the other side of the street to avoid walking too close to Somali neighbors. I've seen folks desperately avoid the homeless man with his sign (I'm guilty of that). In my younger days, I'd often go out of my way to avoid the cross-dresser who would come into the grocery store where I worked.

Pause for a moment to think about all the people who make you uncomfortable. Be honest, and take at least a few moments before continuing.

Imagine one day you come upon a group of people and you realize it includes all of the folks you tend to exclude—all of the people that make you uncomfortable. Imagine that you walk up to the group and notice, in the middle of those gathered, Jesus. He is laughing and has his arm around the shoulders of someone you'd find particularly contemptible.

Jesus included the unclean (even the ones you would exclude). With his love they were rendered clean. And he rarely, if ever, put any conditions upon his inclusion.

THE PEOPLE OF THE TABLE

The New Testament makes little sense if you are unfamiliar with the practice of table fellowship. Paul saved some of his harshest critiques for those who abused the common table—saying that, because of their lack of love for one another, they ate at a "table of demons" instead of the Table of the Lord. Jesus was condemned because of who he ate with. His adversaries couldn't tolerate his sullying himself by eating with "sinners." Likewise,

4. Ibid., 81.

the church was expected to practice hospitality to the stranger—to gather strangers around the table.

The posture of our way of life as the church is, in some ways, summarized by the Table. The Table is the place of mutuality and respect for our sisters and brothers. The Table is the place where we welcome the outsider. And the Table is the place where we leave the comfort of our own home to dine with "sinners."

Hospitality is at the heart of Christianity. And, by definition, it is practiced with strangers. Sharing food and shelter and laughter with friends and family is good, but it isn't hospitality. The word *hospitality* comes from the Latin root *hospes*, which means "stranger" or "guest." It can also, in some instances, mean "host." The Greek word for hospitality is *philoxenos*. This is, incidentally, the word for hospitality we find in the New Testament. *Philo* means "love" and *xenos* means "stranger"—but it can also mean "host." And so, *philoxenos* can mean both "love for the stranger" and "love from the host."

In ancient Greece, practicing hospitality was tied to Zeus, the chief deity. Folks referred to him as *Xenios Zeus*—Zeus the Stranger. The idea was that any stranger could be Zeus in disguise. This myth served to stress the utmost importance of hospitality. Hosts were to welcome the stranger, wash their feet, offer food and wine, and—only after the guest was comfortable—ask the stranger's name.

These linguistic and historical tidbits point to the reality that hospitality, in its ancient sense, isn't simply about welcoming a stranger, but it is also about equalizing the guest and the host. A host who begrudgingly showed care to a guest was considered a poor host. Hosts were to treat guests as equals and help them feel comfortable before even asking their name.

Early Christians were certainly shaped by the Greco-Roman ideas of hospitality. But, just as importantly, they were shaped by Hebrew ideas as well.

The ancient Israelites were to care for strangers and foreigners living among them. The Bible commanded as much. And when the needy and the foreigner weren't cared for, it was grounds for divine judgment.

Within the larger arc of the story of Israel, it was assumed that aliens could become faithful citizens of Israel. In a way the ultimate hospitality of God and his people was the ability for outsiders to be included. It is, arguably, for that reason that God set Israel apart as a sign to the nations.

Both Hebraic and Greco-Roman ideas of hospitality influence Jesus and the early church. In Jesus' teachings, we go from the myth of entertaining Zeus to believing that entertaining strangers is the same as entertaining Jesus. For example, in the chilling sheep-and-goats section of Matthew 25, Jesus reminds us, "Whatever you did for one of the least of these brothers and sisters of mine, you did for me" (v. 40). However, Jesus not only challenged how we extend hospitality but also broke the social norms by being a guest of questionable hosts. He demonstrates radical inclusivity by modeling what it means to be both a guest and a host.

There is little doubt that practicing hospitality gets back to the roots of early Christian practice. But, by itself, it isn't transformative. It is important, in our doing of hospitality, that we not embrace the conceit that simply by feeding the hungry, housing the homeless, or giving aid to those in need, we are destroying social barriers. The world is filled with practitioners of hospitality who, even after years of charitable work, are condescending. It is relatively easy to practice hospitality without embracing justice. Christian hospitality is often radical but rarely revolutionary.

If we the church are to be a people of hospitality—a people of welcome—then we must answer the call to leave our places of safety to bring healing into brokenness. This way of life is clearly seen in Jesus' patterns of ministry.

It is easy to minister to "them," to those whom we judge as "less" than us, but it is hard to see them (and treat them) as family. This is why so much hospitality is materially helpful but spiritually condescending. Paul knew this reality all too well—he was constantly challenging the churches throughout the empire to love one another like family. Nevertheless, the Gentiles judged the Jews and the Jews judged the Gentiles. And the wealthy disrespected the poor (though, interestingly, we don't hear about the poor disrespecting the wealthy).

The Table is a place without judgment. It is a place of acceptance and mutuality. It is a place where all of us come before God just as we are to experience God's presence in and through one another. Jesus' way of hospitality goes way beyond welcome. It moves beyond transaction to transformation. The ultimate goal of hospitality in the way of Jesus is tearing down the walls of division.

That is why Paul had such strong words for the Corinthian church, essentially arguing that when we bring social divisions to our dining room table, we are eating judgment. The Eucharist—the holy meal of the gathered saints—is a revolutionary sacrament. It isn't magical; by eating bread and wine we don't simply become like Jesus. Rather, it is a place where we can reimagine our shared humanity in such a way that we can then go forth and infect the world with healing and liberation.

Around the common table, we are to undo prejudices, judgments, and inequities. Hospitality provides not only an opportunity to attend to basic needs but also a chance to destroy the very inequities that render such attention necessary.

The question is, How do we embody God's heart? Can we be a people who sit at table with strangers and let the walls of division fall? Can we gather together and allow the Spirit to weave us into one new people? How do we take everything that is ours and yield them to God's dream for us? How do we welcome the stranger as Christ and be a willing guest in uncomfortable places? We must give and receive revolutionary hospitality.

Revolutionary hospitality refuses to accept the status quo. It moves beyond mere charity and instead creates space for enemies to live as family, strangers to live as friends. It challenges the assumption that some are more important than others. Celebrity and hierarchy and power-over are undone at the revolutionary table.

I believe this begins with hospitality—by inviting people into our common lives in such a way that our most basic understanding of family and community is transformed. Hospitality becomes revolutionary when the line between the host and the guest, the owner and the dispossessed, the master and the slave, the privileged and the marginalized gets so blurred that we can begin to redefine our social relations in the way of Jesus Christ.

When we gather around the table, we can experience Jesus Christ through our friends, through strangers, and even through enemies. And we can begin to become the body of Christ, showing God's love to an inhospitable world.

CHAPTER NINE GROUP GUIDE

 Summary

If we take Jesus seriously, we will reorganize our social lives. Communities of faith must move beyond talking about Jesus to embodying what Jesus taught, putting into practice among the few what we long for among the many. If we believe in justice, then we must embody justice, beginning with the people we see on the street and encounter at the table of communion.

 Discussion Questions

1. How can we live more deeply into the practice of hospitality?
2. Who are the sorts of people we'd be least likely to welcome at this table?
3. How can we use our resources to meet the deepest needs in our midst?
4. What do we hope will come from studying these nine chapters together?

 Group Practice

In this final study group together, prepare a simple meal. Try to let everyone play a part in creating the meal—through food preparation, setting the table, doing the dishes, etc. As you eat together, engage the discussion questions.

 Close with a time of silence or prayer.

Suggested Resources

Loaves and Fishes, by Dorothy Day
Making Room: Recovering Hospitality as a Christian Tradition, by Christine Pohl
Unclean: Meditations on Purity, Hospitality, and Morality, by Richard Beck
Babette's Feast (film)

Conclusion:
When Repentance Becomes Revolution

Jesus is dead in the buildings and in the cities and in the outside.
But he is alive in our hearts.

—St. Jonas of Minneapolis

I WANT TO THANK you for walking with me through the pages of this book. It certainly isn't a "feel-good" book—at least superficially. Yet I believe we can find hope in repentance. That we never come to the end of repentance—of turning away from the old world as we step with fragility into the new. That can be a discouraging thought, because our hearts long for utopia.

But it can be a hopeful thing, knowing that there is always a deeper reality to step into. In the words of the unicorn at the end of C. S. Lewis' *Last Battle*, "I have come home at last! This is my real country! I belong here. This is the land I have been looking for all my life, though I never knew it till now . . . Come further up, come further in!"[1] The call to repentance is our call to go further up and further into the deep reality of God.

This task is deeply mystical, intensely personal, and highly political. The intermingling of these categories can raise anxiety. As I wrote this book, people would ask, "What's your book about?" Often, I would say, "Well, it is a call to embrace Jesus' mystical anarchism." Such a description hardly conjures the cozy reading of books by a warm fire, with hot cocoa within easy reach.

So while this book isn't cozy, I have found writing it to be a comfort. My hope is that all those who read this book—those who, I suspect, are

---

1. Lewis, *Last Battle*, 196.

discontent with the world as it is—may find comfort in the revolutionary provocations I've tried to articulate.

In the end, this book is an invitation to Catholic Worker cofounder Peter Maurin's dream "to build a new society in the shell of the old." To build this new society requires a mystical vision wherein we believe that God can tear down the walls that imprison us. To build this new society requires new eyes and a strange willingness to be dismissed as a fool. There is a wild foolishness in embracing the unKingdom of God.

Paulo Freire, in his revolutionary work *Pedagogy of the Oppressed*, suggests that whenever we act in this world in truth, we change the world. This is why mysticism and radical action must go together. To act in truth requires that we first see in truth. But to see the truth, we must have started walking in the way of truth. There is a paradox here that can only be resolved by heeding Philip's call to "come and see" (John 1:46).

May we listen to the prophetic call to repent as we step into the mystical call to see the world with new eyes. And then, as we step into the new world (the unKingdom of God), the world is changed.

This is potentially revolutionary. According to anarchist anthropologist David Graeber,

> Revolutionary action is any collective action which rejects, and therefore confronts, some form of power or domination and in doing so, reconstitutes social relations—even within the collectivity—in that light. Revolutionary action does not necessarily have to aim to topple governments. Attempts to create autonomous communities in the face of power . . . would, for instance, be almost by definition revolutionary acts. And history shows us that the continual accumulation of such acts can change (almost) everything.[2]

Revolution doesn't begin with the seizing of power or the toppling of governments, or even in the rising tides of anger. It begins with love. This is how repentance becomes revolution. As we pray "God, may we give up for love's sake even what you has given us." As we walk into the new world that we are creating together with the Spirit, a new world inaugurated by Jesus Christ. This new world is the unKingdom of God.

---

2. Graeber, *Fragments*, 45.

Bibliography

The Ante-Nicene Fathers. Edited by Alexander Roberts and James Donaldson. 1885–87. 10 vols. Reprint, New York: Scribner's, 1899.

Armitage, David. *The Ideological Origins of the British Empire*. Cambridge: Cambridge University Press, 2000.

Bauckham, Richard. *The Bible and Ecology: Rediscovering the Community of Creation*. Waco, TX: Baylor University Press, 2010.

Beck, Richard. *Unclean: Meditations on Purity, Hospitality, and Morality*. Eugene, OR: Cascade, 2011.

Brueggemann, Walter. *The Prophetic Imagination*. 2nd ed. Minneapolis: Fortress, 2001.

Colby, Gerard, and Charlotte Dennett. *Thy Will Be Done: The Conquest of the Amazon; Nelson Rockefeller and Evangelism in the Age of Oil*. New York: HarperCollins, 1995.

Cullen, Jim. *The American Dream: A Short History of an Idea That Shaped a Nation*. New York: Oxford University Press, 2003.

Drake, H. A. *Constantine and the Bishops*. Baltimore: Johns Hopkins University Press, 2002.

Ellul, Jacques. *Anarchy and Christianity*. Translated by Geoffrey W. Bromiley. Grand Rapids: Eerdmans, 1991.

———. *The New Demons*. Translated by C. Edward Hopkin. New York: Seabury, 1975.

Endo, Shusaku. *Silence*. Translated by William Johnston. New York: Taplinger, 1980.

Freire, Paulo. *Pedagogy of the Oppressed*. Translated by Myra Bergman Ramos. New York: Continuum, 1997.

Gaddis, Michael. *There Is No Crime for Those Who Have Christ: Religious Violence in the Christian Roman Empire*. Berkeley: University of California Press, 2015.

Girard, René. *I See Satan Fall Like Lightning*. Translated by James G. Williams. Maryknoll, NY: Orbis, 2001.

Graeber, David. *Fragments of an Anarchist Anthropology*. Chicago: Prickly Paradigm, 2004.

Haffner, Hans. *Concerning a True Soldier of Christ*. *Mennonite Quarterly Review* 5 (1931).

Hardt, Michael, and Antonio Negri. *Empire*. Cambridge: Harvard University Press, 2000.

Howard-Brook, Wes. *"Come Out, My People!": God's Call out of Empire in the Bible and Beyond*. Maryknoll, NY: Orbis, 2012.

Howard-Brook, Wes, and Anthony Gwyther. *Unveiling Empire: Reading Revelation Then and Now*. Maryknoll, NY: Orbis, 1999.

Kazantzakis, Nikos. *Report to Greco*. Translated by P. A. Bien. London: Faber & Faber, 2001.

Kinsler, Gloria, and Ross Kinsler. *The Biblical Jubilee and the Struggle for Life: An Invitation to Personal, Ecclesial, and Social Transformation*. Maryknoll, NY: Orbis, 1999.

Levine, Bruce. *Get Up, Stand Up: Uniting Populists, Engergizing the Defeated, and Battling the Corporate Elite*. White River Junction, VT: Chelsea Green, 2011.

Lewis, C. S. *The Last Battle*. New York: Harper, 1956.

Macy, Joanna, and Molly Young Brown. *Coming Back to Life: The Updated Guide to the Work That Reconnects*. Gabriola Island, BC: New Society, 1998.

Mitchell, Roger Haydon. *Church, Gospel, and Empire: How the Politics of Sovereignty Impregnated the West*. Eugene, OR: Wipf & Stock, 2011.

Myers, Ched. "The Fall." In *The Encyclopedia of Religion and Nature*, edited by Bron Taylor et al., 1:634–36. London: Thoemmes Continuum, 2005.

——. "To Serve and Preserve." *Sojourners*, March 2004. http://sojo.net/magazine/2004/03/serve-and-preserve.

Postman, Neil. *Amusing Ourselves to Death*. New York: Penguin, 1985.

Schüssler Fiorenza, Elisabeth. *The Power of the Word: Scripture and the Rhetoric of Empire*. Minneapolis: Fortress, 2007.

Sharlet, Jeff. *C Street: The Fundamentalist Threat to American Democracy*. Boston: Little, Brown, 2010.

Sölle, Dorothee. *Beyond Mere Obedience*. Translated by Lawrence W. Denef. New York: Pilgrim, 1982.

——. *Suffering*. Translated by Everett R. Kalin. Philadelphia: Fortress, 1975.

——. *The Silent Cry: Mysticism and Resistance*. Translated by Barbara and Martin Rumscheidt. Minneapolis: Fortress, 2001.

Stark, Rodney. *The Rise of Christianity*. San Francisco: HarperSanFrancisco, 1997.

Stringfellow, William. *An Ethic for Christians and Other Aliens in a Strange Land*. 1973. Reprint, Eugene, OR: Wipf & Stock, 2004.

——. *A Private and Public Faith*. Grand Rapids: Eerdmans, 1962.

Underhill, Evelyn. *Mysticism: A Study in the Nature and Development of Spiritual Consciousness*. 1930. Reprint, Mineola, NY: Dover, 2002.

Weil, Simone. *On Science, Necessity, and the Love of God: Essays*. Collected, translated, and edited by Richard Rees. Oxford: Oxford University Press, 1968.

Williams, Edwin, ed. *Addresses and Messages of the Presidents of the United States, Inaugural, Annual, and Special, from 1789 to 1846*. Vol. 2. New York: Edward Walker, 1846.

Wink, Walter. *Engaging the Powers*. Minneapolis: Fortress, 1992.

——. *Naming the Powers*. Philadelphia: Fortress, 1984.

Wright, N. T. *Jesus and the Victory of God*. Minneapolis: Fortress, 1997.

——. "The New Testament and the 'State.'" *Themelios* 16 (1990) 11–17.

Yoder, John Howard. *Body Politics: Five Practices of the Christian Community before the Watching World*. Scottsdale, PA: Herald, 2001.

——. *The Politics of Jesus: Vicit Agnus Noster*. Grand Rapids: Eerdmans, 1994.

Made in the USA
Columbia, SC
30 July 2022

64341288R00093